Tax Aspects of Corporate Division

Tax Aspects of Corporate Division

W. Eugene Seago

BEP

BUSINESS EXPERT PRESS

Leader in applied, concise business books

Tax Aspects of Corporate Division
Copyright © Business Expert Press, LLC, 2021.

First published in 2021 by
Business Expert Press, LLC
222 East 46th Street, New York, NY 10017
www.businessexpertpress.com

ISBN-13: 978-1-95334-940-8 (paperback)
ISBN-13: 978-1-95334-941-5 (e-book)

Business Expert Press Financial Accounting, Auditing, and Taxation
Collection

Collection ISSN: 2151-2795 (print)
Collection ISSN: 2151-2817 (electronic)

Cover design by Charlene Kronstedt
Interior design by S4Carlisle Publishing Services Private Ltd., Chennai,
India

First edition: 2021

10 9 8 7 6 5 4 3 2 1

Printed in the United States of America.

Description

For a variety of reasons, corporations can achieve business efficiencies by dividing into two or more entities. The tax consequences of the division could be that both the corporation and the shareholders must recognize taxable income, which often renders the division unfeasible.

In order to neutralize the tax effects of business-motivated decisions to divide the corporation, the tax law provides the means for the division to be accomplished without immediate tax consequences for the corporation and its shareholders. The enabling provisions are necessarily complex so as to prevent their exploitation and bring together several other corporate tax concepts dealing with dividends and reorganizations. Moreover, the rules have often changed.

This book explains and illustrates each of the requirements for a nontaxable corporate division and the methods for mitigating the tax consequences when those requirements cannot be satisfied. The author also provides numerous diagrams that summarize actual transactions.

Keywords

tax; corporate division; shareholders; corporate tax; tax rules; finance; loss; gain; tax consequences

Contents

Preface

In a variety of circumstances management of a corporation may have good business reasons for dividing the corporation into two or more corporations in such a manner that shareholders in the original corporation own stock in each of the resulting entities. This may mean that assets must be moved from one corporate shell to another and stock must be distributed to the shareholders. Thus, under the general rules of taxation, the original corporation and their shareholders would realize taxable income. However, under certain conditions the realized gains are not taxed at the time of the distribution or exchange.

This book discusses the reasons the Internal Revenue Code provisions governing corporate division were first added to law, how the law was used and abused, and then how it was changed to curb the perceived abuses. The tax laws establish the conditions under which the division may occur without the recognition of gain by the corporation and the shareholders: These conditions relate to the business purpose, and continuity of investment, which are generally required for corporate restructuring. However, a corporate division provides opportunities for abuses of the laws. Any corporate management contemplating a division must be aware of the statutory safeguards against abuse built into the law, whether or not any abuse is intended.

Chapter 1 of this book briefly discusses the development of the tax rules related to corporate division. Chapters 2,3,4, 5 and 6 discuss specific requirements the division must satisfy to gain the preferred tax treatment for the shareholder and the corporation. Chapters 7 and 8 discuss more recent changes in the law that may require the distributing corporation to recognize gain when the shareholder is not taxed on the transactions. Chapter 9 serves as a review of the materials in the other chapters by discussing specific factual situations where the law has been applied.

As will be seen, corporate division often brings into play a variety of corporate tax laws, including distributions, reorganizations, stock redemptions and consolidated tax returns. Moreover, a corporate division is often integrated with other transactions, which creates issues about which steps must be considered in evaluating the corporate division. Thus, guiding clients through a corporate division requires the application of the practitioner's cumulate knowledge and skills. Corporate division is where the practitioner must "put it all together."

CHAPTER 1

Corporate Division: Uses and Abuses

Introduction

This book is about the tax consequence of dividing a corporation into two or more corporate entities. The division usually takes the form of a spin-off, split-off, or a split-up.

In a *spin-off*, a corporation distributes to its shareholders a controlling in the stock of a subsidiary. In another form of a spin-off, a corporation may transfer some of its assets to a newly formed corporation in exchange for all of the corporation's stock, which the parent corporation distributes to its shareholders. For the shareholder, the spin-off is equivalent to a dividend in the form of stock in another corporation, and for the distributing corporation, the spin-off is economically equivalent to paying a dividend to its shareholders in the form of stock in another corporation.

A *split-off* is the same as a *spin-off*, except that not all of the shareholders participate: That is, the parent corporation transfers its stock that is a controlling interest in a subsidiary to one or a limited group of its shareholders in exchange for their stock in the distributing corporation. The split-off is essentially a stock redemption.

A *split-up* is similar to a spin-off, except that all the assets of a corporation are divided between two new corporations in exchange for all of their stock. Then the original corporation distributes to its shareholders the stock in the two corporations, and the original corporation dissolves. For the shareholders, the split-up is similar to a stock dividend.

In each of these three types of transactions, the corporation and the shareholders have altered their property rights through exchanges and distributions. Therefore, under the general rules of taxation, realized gains or losses must be recognized.[1] However, the tax law contains specific rules for these transactions that provide the corporation the unique ability to distribute property to its shareholders without the corporation and its shareholders incurring a tax liability.

Rationale for the Exception

The Spin-Off

In a multitude of situations, corporate management may determine that for good business reasons, the shareholders should directly own the corporation's subsidiary or that the corporation should be divided into two or more corporations. If the general rules for the taxation of corporations and their shareholders were applied, a substantial tax burden could accompany the implementation of the business decision. Thus, the tax laws would not be neutral in regard to this type of business decision. The lack of neutrality in the tax laws can also work in the other direction: That is, the tax laws can also create benefits such that actions will be undertaken primarily to achieve the tax benefit, rather than to achieve a business purpose. Thus, over the past 100 years, the tax laws regarding corporate division have undergone substantial changes in an attempt to make the tax laws neutral in the sense of not interfering with business-motivated decisions but without creating tax-motivated transactions.

The need to neutralize the tax laws in regard to business decisions is illustrated by an early case, *Rockefeller v. United States*,[2] where a vertically integrated oil company produced, refined, and transported (through its pipelines) petroleum products. The transportation business was subject to regulatory controls that complicated the other corporate operations. These complications could be eliminated by transferring the transportation business to a newly formed subsidiary corporation and distributing the stock to the parent corporation's shareholders. Therefore, the oil company created a new corporation and transferred the transportation assets to the new corporation in exchange for all of the new corporation's stock, which was distributed to the oil company shareholders. Thus, the

---

[1] *Cottage Savings Association v. Commissioner*, 499 U.S. 554 (1991).
[2] 257 U.S. 176 (1921).

shareholders previously owned a corporation that included the transportation and oil production businesses, and after the transactions, the shareholders owned stock in two corporations conducting the same businesses formerly combined in one corporation. The Court noted that the shareholders did not experience an increase in wealth as a result of receiving the stock. This was true because the value of parent corporation that included the oil and transportation assets was equal to the sum of the value of the oil business retained by the parent and the new corporation with the transportation assets.[3] Moreover, the shareholders continued their investment, although in a different form, but the shareholder's legal rights changed from indirect to direct owners of the transportation business. Thus, for example, as a result of the distribution of the transportation business stock, the individual shareholder could sell his or her ownership in the transportation business but keep the oil stock, which was not possible when both businesses were lodged in one corporation. At the time of the distribution, the changes in property rights resulting from the distribution of the transportation corporation stock met the tax definition of a corporate dividend, which was taxable income to the shareholder as an increase in wealth that had been realized.[4]

Some shareholders in *Rockefeller* may have depended upon the corporate dividends for their ordinary living expenses. The tax on the value of the stock distributed could necessitate the shareholder selling some of the stock to pay the tax. However, the stock sale could give rise to more tax on the gain and, thus, it would be necessary to sell more stock, which, in turn, would create a still greater tax liability. The point is that it was not difficult to build the case that taxing the spin-off that was compelled by government regulations, rather than to achieve a tax objective, would be bad tax policy. Moreover, if the division was based on a valid business reason and the benefit the shareholder enjoyed from the distribution was the ability to sell stock in one of the businesses and retain the ownership interest in the other business, but the shareholder did not sell the stock in either corporation, why penalize the shareholders? Therefore,

---

[3]Corporate management often justifies the corporate division as increasing shareholder value by, for example, separating risky assets.

[4]*Eisner v. Macomber*, 252 U.S. 189 (1920).

Congress enacted laws to create the nontaxable spin-off to counter the results reached in *Rockefeller* and other similar cases.

The Second Circuit of the U.S. Court of Appeals has interpreted the legislative history of the spin-off as follows:

> Its [the spin-off] purpose is to give to stockholders in a corporation controlled by them the privilege of separating or 'spinning off' from their corporation a part of its assets and activities and lodging the separated part in another corporation which is controlled by the same stockholders. Since, after the spin-off, the real owners of the assets are the same persons who owned them before, Congress has been willing that these real owners should be allowed, **without penalty**, to have their real ownership divided into smaller artificial entities than the single original corporation, if the real owners decide that such a division would be desirable.[5]

The Supreme Court has summarized the underlying objective of the tax rules for corporate divisions as follows: "the general purpose of [the spin-off rules] was to distinguish corporate fission from the distribution of [the corporation's] earnings and profits."[6] Thus, the division of an existing corporation, which requires the corporation to distribute stock to shareholders who continue their investment, is worthy of distinction from the common dividend.

The Split-Off

Congress also enacted laws allowing the nontaxable split-off for situations as existed in *W. E. Gabriel Fabrication Co.*[7] Two brothers each owned 50 percent of the stock in one corporation but could not agree on how to operate the business. Their inability to agree on business matters adversely affected the business operations. The brothers decided to split the business and go their separate ways. To accomplish the separation, some of the assets of their equally owned corporation were transferred to a newly

---

[5] *Parshelsky's Estate v. Commissioner*, 303 F.2d 14 (1962).
[6] *Commissioner v. Gordon.* 391 U.S. 83, 92 (1968).
[7] 42 T.C. 545 (1964).

formed corporation in exchange for 100 percent of its stock. Then, one of the brothers gave up all of his stock in the original corporation in exchange for all of the stock in the newly formed corporation. These transactions taken together could satisfy the requirements for a nontaxable "split-off." On the other hand, without the benefit of tax statutes authorizing the split-off without immediate tax consequences, the original corporation and the exiting brother would have taxable income, and such a tax burden could deter the brothers from extricating themselves from a contentious business relationship: The tax laws would not be neutral in regard to their business decision.

Other Uses of the Spin-Off and Split-Off

One commentator noted that corporate "divisions are almost never mere divisions. Distributing [the corporation making the distribution of a subsidiary] may acquire a trade or business to spin; a person may acquire Distributing stock to receive a spinoff or split-off; Controlled [the stock distributed]… may issue up to 20 percent of its stock to raise cash; or Distributing or Controlled may just want to become nubile to be a more attractive acquisition partner."[8] Thus, the spin-off or split-off is frequently a part of a plan involving other corporate transactions. Often, the division is used to dispose of "unwanted" assets; that is, a corporation that is an acquisition target may have specific assets that the acquiror does not want or cannot afford. A spin-off may enable the target corporation to dispose of the unwanted assets without the immediate effects of the double taxation of corporate income.

The System of Double Taxation

In General

The tax rules for corporate division are based on a fundamental principle that corporate income should ultimately be subject to tax at the corporate and shareholder levels: The corporation should be taxed on the income

---

[8]J.L. Cummings, Jr., Spinning, Acquiring, and Disposing, *Tax Notes*, January 1, 2018, p. 101.

when it is recognized as earned, and the shareholder should be taxed when the corporate income is distributed. The rules for corporate division will defer income in the appropriate situations, but should not eliminate taxable income experienced by the corporation and its shareholders.

When appreciated property is distributed to the shareholder, the corporation generally must recognize income from the distribution equal to the excess of the fair market value of the asset distributed over the corporation's basis in the asset,[9] and the shareholder must recognize dividend income equal to the fair market value of the asset distributed.[10] As an important exception to this scheme, for certain transactions that qualify as corporate spin-offs or split-offs, where the stock in a subsidiary is distributed to the parent's shareholders, the shareholder's and the corporation's realized gains are deferred.

> Example: P Corporation has accumulated earnings and profits of $75 when P distributed property with a value of $100 and P's basis was $60. Under the general rules, P would have a taxable $40 gain ($100 value − $60 basis); the shareholder will recognize dividend income of $100, and the shareholder's basis in the distributed property will be $100. Thus, the $40 appreciation in value would be taxed at the corporate and shareholder levels at the time of the distribution.

Assume that in the above example, P's distribution is the stock of P's wholly owned subsidiary, S Inc., and the distribution qualified as a nontaxable spin-off (i.e., the shareholders receive all of the S stock in proportion to their P stock):

- P does not recognize the $40 realized gain.[11]
- The P shareholders do not recognize dividend income.[12]

---

[9]Section 311(b).

[10]The shareholder's income is limited to the corporation's earnings and profits (generally, the sum of the corporation's after tax income less distributions for all years.)

[11]Section 355(c).

[12]Section 355(a)(1).

- The P shareholder allocates a portion of his or her basis in the P stock as basis in the S stock.[13]
- The spun-off corporation does not recognize gain or loss, and the bases in its assets do not change as a result of the distribution.

As a spin-off, the corporation whose stock is distributed, the subsidiary, generally does not recognize gain until it sells its assets, but the distributing corporation is never taxed on the appreciation in the assets of the spun-off corporation while the distributing corporation owned the distributed stock. Thus, the system defers and shifts income among corporations and shareholders, but ultimately does not exclude income from taxation.

Avoiding Triple Taxation

In the previous example, the corporation distributed property with a basis of $60 and a fair market value of $100. If section 355 did not apply the distributing corporation was required to recognize $40 gain. If section 355 did not apply the shareholder was required to recognize $100 dividend income. The shareholder's income was a distribution of the corporation's earnings and profits; generally, the corporation's accumulated after-tax income that included the corporation's $40 realized gain from the distribution. Thus, the $40 appreciation in the value of the property distributed was taxed twice. Assume that the property distributed was stock in another corporation that was distributed to an individual shareholder and that the difference between the value of the stock distributed and the distributing corporation's basis was all attributable to appreciation in the assets of the corporation whose stock was distributed. The distributing corporation and the shareholder will include the $40 appreciation in income, but the corporation whose stock was distributed will have a built-in gain of $40 that will be taxed win the corporation sells its assets; thus, the $40 appreciation will be taxed three times, when, under the general system of taxation, the corporate income should be taxed twice.

_____

[13]Section 358(b)(2).

When the distributing corporation distributes a controlling interest (generally 80 percent of the stock in the controlled corporation) and the distribution satisfies the requirements of section 355, triple taxation of the corporate income is avoided, as explained above. However, if the section 355 requirements are not satisfied, then the distribution will be taxable to the distributing corporation and the shareholder, but the corporation whose stock is distributed may have built-in gains (i.e., the value of its assets is greater than their basis). In such a case, the parties must go to extra lengths to avoid triple taxation. The corporations can elect under section 336(e) or 338(h)(10)[14] to tax the controlled corporation on the appreciation in its assets and the corporation can write-up the bases in its assets, but the distributing corporation is not taxed.

Example: P Corporation owns 100 percent of the T Corporation stock with a value of $100, and P's basis in the stock is $60. T's basis in its assets is $60. P distributed the T stock to its shareholders, and the requirements of section 355 were not satisfied. P must recognized a taxable $40 gain ($100 value − $60 basis); the shareholder will recognize dividend income of $100, and the shareholder's basis in the distributed property will be $100. Thus, the $40 appreciation in value has been taxed at the corporate and shareholder levels at the time of the distribution and T has a built-in gain (FMV of assets–basis) of $40.

Instead of applying the general rules, an election was made under section 336(e) or section 338(h)(10) if the controlling interest is sold to a corporation. Under the election, P is not taxed on its $40 realized gain, but the P shareholders are taxed. T is taxed on the $40 built-in gain and its basis in the assets is increase at $100. Thus, the $40 gain will be taxed twice, rather than being taxed three times.

The Form of the Transactions

The Spin-off in the previous example, P and S were a parent and its subsidiary when P's management decided for business reasons to distribute the S stock to the P shareholders. However, assume that P owned appreciated

---

[14]The election is made in accordance with the section 338(h)(10) regulations if another corporation receives a controlling interest in the distributed stock; otherwise, the election is made under the section 336(e) regulations.

business assets, but P's management decided the business should be under the direct control of the P shareholders. A direct distribution of the assets would result in taxable gain to P and dividend income to the P shareholders. To avoid this immediate tax, P could transfer the assets to Newco, its newly created subsidiary, and then distribute the Newco stock to the P shareholders, as in the previous example. While generally the transfer of property to the subsidiary in exchange for stock could be nontaxable (a transfer of property to a corporation controlled by the transferor, under section 351), the problem would be that P would lose control following the distribution of the Newco stock and, thus, the transfers to Newco could be a taxable transaction. However, if the Code requirements for a spin-off or split-off are satisfied, the transfer of assets and distribution of subsidiary stock can qualify as a section 368(a)(1)(D) reorganization and P and its shareholders will not recognize income—the same result as when the assets were already in a preexisting subsidiary. The spin-off and split-off transactions are illustrated in Figure 1.1 and 1.2, respectively.

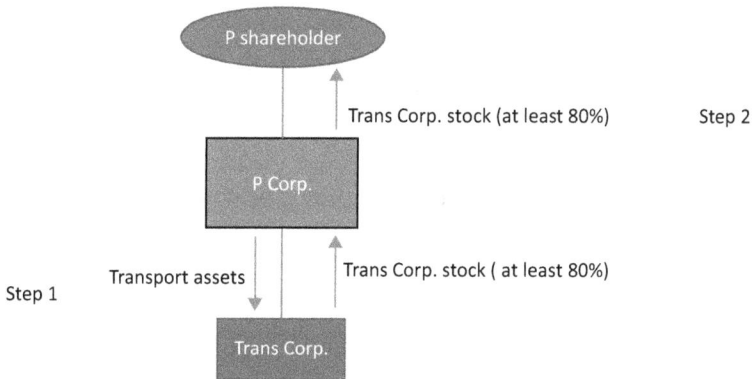

Figure 1.1 The Rockefeller Spin-Off: **P Corporation transferred its transportation assets to a new corporation and distributed the stock to its shareholders**

B gives up his 50 percent of P Corporation stock for all of the Trans The Split-off, stock.

It should be noted that in the split-off, as in *Gabriel* (discussed above), the transaction can become complex because of differences in the value of the stock being surrendered and the stock being received. For example, in *Gabriel*, the value of his stock in P may have been $50, but the value

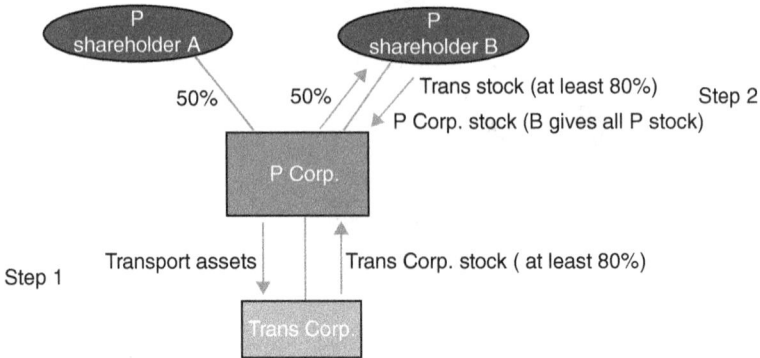

Figure 1.2 *The Gabriel Split-Off* begins with A and B each owning 50 percent of the P Corporation stock

of the transportation assets to be distributed in exchange for the P stock may have been only $40. Therefore, it may be necessary for P to transfer additional assets to Trans Corporation to even-up the valuations, or P Corporation may need to pay B cash for the other 20 percent of value of his stock, which would require B to recognize any realized gain, but not more than the cash (or other property other than stock) received,[15] or, as another possibility, P could transfer an additional $10 cash to bring the value of the subsidiary to equal the value of B's 50 percent interest in P.

Second-Tier Subsidiary Spin-Off

In the *Rockefeller* spin-off, the parent corporation transferred assets to a subsidiary (controlled) in exchange for a controlling interest in the subsidiary's stock. Then the parent distributed the stock in the controlled corporation to the parent's shareholders. If the parent already controlled a subsidiary, the controlling interest could be distributed directly to the parent's shareholders. The parent's shareholders in the example were all assumed to be individuals. As a result, the organizational structure changed from parent-subsidiary, where one corporation controlled another corporation, to brother–sister, where the same group of shareholders control two different corporations.

---

[15]Section 356(a).

However, spin-offs are often a means of rearranging ownership within a group of corporations. Often, the parent has a (first-tier) subsidiary that has its own (second-tier) subsidiary, and for good business reasons, the upper tier parent desires to have direct control over the second-tier subsidiary. This can be achieved by the first-tier subsidiary distributing the second-tier subsidiary stock to the Parent (Figure 1.3).

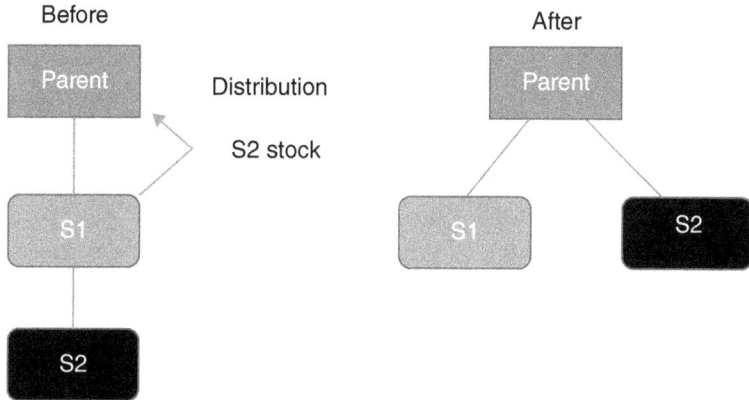

Figure 1.3 **Spin-off of a second-tier subsidiary**

The distribution to the Parent is either (1) a nontaxable spin-off or (2) a distribution (dividend) by S1 to its corporate parent.[16] If the distribution satisfies the requirements of section 355 (discussed below), it will be nontaxable corporate division and neither Parent nor S1 will recognized income; moreover, the parent will allocate its basis in S1 stock between the S1 and the S2 stock. If the section 355 requirements are not satisfied, the transactions will be accounted for as a dividend paid by S1 to Parent. As a dividend, and assuming the corporations file a consolidated return,[17]

- Neither S1 nor the Parent will recognize income from the S1 to Parent distribution.
- Parent will reduce its basis in the S2 stock by the value of the S2 stock.

---

[16]See section 355(f) discussed later in these materials.

[17]See Reg. §1.1502-3(f) (7), Example 1.

- S1 will have a deferred intercompany gain equal to the excess of the value of the S2 stock over S1's basis.
- S1's will recognize the deferred gain when Parent distributes or sells the S2 stock.[18]
- S2 will not recognize income and its bases in its assets are unchanged.

Example: P, S1, and S2 file consolidated returns. P ownw 100 percent of the S1 stock and S1 owns 100 percent of the S2 stock. P's basis in S1 is $250, and S1's basis in the S2 stock is $70 when S1 distributed 100 percent of the S2 stock to P. Neither P nor S1 recognize income. P must reduce its basis in the S1 stock by its fair market value, $100, P must reduce its basis in the S1 stock by $100. S1 has a deferred intercompany gain of $100 − $70 = $30. S1 must recognize the deferred gain whenever S1 leaves the consolidated group or P sells or distributes the S2 stock.

Assume P distributed the S2 stock when its value was $110: S1 must recognize the $30 deferred gain, and P must recognize $110 − $100 = $10 gain.

Recap of the Tax Effects of Spin-Offs and Split-Offs

A spin-off that satisfied the certain (to be discussed) requirements is non-taxable to the distributing corporation and its shareholders, and the shareholder's basis in the distributing corporation must be allocated between the basis in the distributing corporation and the distributed stock.[19] If the "certain requirements" are not satisfied, the distribution of the stock is taxed as a dividend to the shareholders (to the extent of the corporation's earnings and profits) and recognized taxable gain to the corporation, if appreciated property is distributed. The character of the shareholder's income (i.e., ordinary or capital) from the split-off is determined by applying the stock redemption rules.[20] The character of the corporation's income depends upon the character whether the property distributed is capital gain or ordinary income property.

---

[18]Reg. §1.1502-13(d), Example 16.

[19]Section 358(b).

[20]Section 302. See *Commissioner v. Clark*, 489 U.S. 726 (1989).

In a split-off, the shareholder exchanges his or her stock in the parent for the stock in the subsidiary, which results in a complete termination of the shareholder's interests in the parent. If certain requirements are satisfied, the shareholder does not recognize gain and his or basis in the parent stock becomes the basis in the subsidiary stock;[21] otherwise, the shareholder will recognize capital gain equal to the excess of the value of the subsidiary stock received over the basis in the parent stock surrendered and will have a fair market value basis in the stock received.

Potential Abuses: When Laws Are Non-neutral in the "Wrong" Direction

As discussed earlier, the tax benefits of the spin-off and split-off are that the corporation and shareholder are allowed to alter their corporate holdings without the shareholder and the corporation recognizing taxable income. Congress realized that businesses often have good business reasons for changing the corporate structure and stock ownership, but if the tax law creates a "toll charge" on the transactions, the desired changes might not occur. Therefore, to neutralize the tax laws in regard to the changes in the corporate structure, under the appropriate circumstances, the taxable income can be deferred. However, soon after enacting the statutes enabling the spin-off, Congress realized that strict limitations on the tax-free transactions were needed. The need for changes in the law were made apparent by the Board of Tax Appeals decision in *Gregory v. Commissioner* (Figure 1.4).[22]

Mrs. Gregory was the sole shareholder in United Mortgage Company, United owned investment assets. Mrs. Gregory's plan was for the investments to be sold, but she would receive the sales proceeds. If United simply sold the stock and distributed the proceeds to her, Mrs. Gregory would have taxable dividends.[23] To avoid the tax, Mrs. Gregory caused United to contribute the investments to a newly formed corporation,

---

[21]Section 358(a).

[22]27 B.T.A. 223 (1932), reversed by *Gregory v. Helvering*, 293 U.S. 465 (1935).

[23]At the time of the distribution, the corporation was not taxed on distributions of appreciated property.

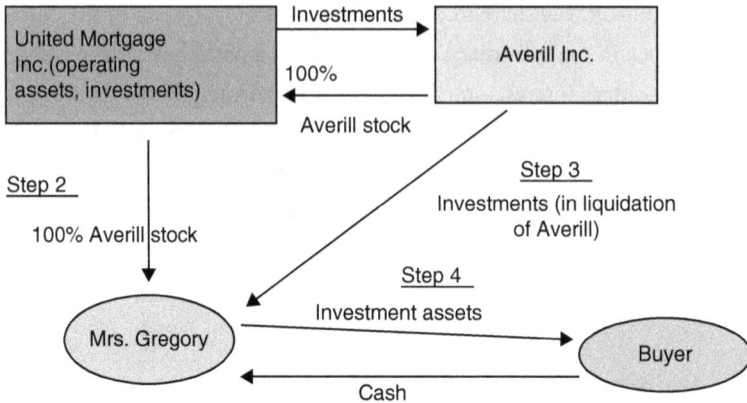

Figure 1.4 **Gregory v. Helvering**

Averill Corporation, for 100 percent of the Averill stock. This was a non-taxable section 351 transaction, and Averill's basis in the investments was the same as United's basis in the investments. Soon after Averill was formed, United distributed the Averill stock to Mrs. Gregory. The formation of Averill and distribution of the stock to Mrs. Gregory met all of the then existing requirements for a tax deferred spin-off, and therefore, Mrs. Gregory recognized no taxable income but was required to allocate her basis in the United Sock between United and Averill. Six days after the spin-off, Averill was liquidated and the investemnts were distributed to Mrs. Gregory, who reported a capital gain from the liquidation (which was treated as a taxable exchange of her Averill stock for the investments) and a fair market value basis in the investments which she sold. Thus, the net of all of these transactions was Mrs. Gregory got value out of Union equal to the fair market value of the investments and the capital gain recognized was the value received less the basis in the United stock allocated to the Averill stock. Under the law as it existed at the time of the transaction, Averill was not required to recognize gain from liquidating.

The Board of Tax Appeals applied a literal interpretation of the statute, which, if allowed to stand, would have meant that a corporation could easily transfer assets to its shareholders without the corporation recognizing income from the appreciation in the asset. The shareholder could avoid tax until the stock received was sold, at which time the shareholder would have capital gain, rather than dividend income. Moreover, the capital gain would be less than the dividend income because the shareholder would have a basis (allocated) in the distributed stock. All that was required to avoid tax was for the corporation to place some of its assets in a corporation it controlled and distribute the stock in the controlled corporation.

But the appellate court believed that merely adhering to the words in the statute was not sufficient.[24] The second circuit opinion by Judge Learned Hand presents a variety of reasons based on existing tax doctrines that the transactions were not worthy of tax-deferred treatment in Mrs. Gregory's case. According to Judge Hand, in addition to meeting the requirements of the statute, the transactions must also satisfy the congressional intent of the law. Here the transactions were purported to constitute a corporate reorganization, and the law exempts "from tax the gain from exchanges made in connection with a reorganization in order that ordinary business transactions will not be prevented." But the transactions as a whole did not satisfy a corporate business purpose, but rather, the transactions were solely designed to create a tax benefit for the shareholder. Moreover, Judge Hand reasoned that the concept of a reorganization implies a continuity of interest by the shareholders, whereas the transactions terminated Mrs. Gregory's interest in Monitor. Also, when the integrated steps are collapsed, in substance, Mrs. Gregory received value from her corporation, United, without reducing her control over the corporation, which was essentially equivalent to a dividend. Thus, the second circuit reversed the Board of Tax Appeals. The Supreme Court affirmed the second circuit, agreeing that the transactions had no corporate business purpose and, therefore, should not qualify for tax-deferred reorganization treatment.[25]

Learned Hand's opinion suggested several rationales for not permitting tax-deferred treatment under the facts of the case: (1) substance over form as determined by collapsing the integrated steps (transactions), (2) lack of business purpose, and (3) lack of the continuity of investment. These arguments against Mrs. Gregory and the corporation recognizing taxable income are discussed in depth later. However, if Mrs. Gregory

---

[24] *Gregory v. Helvering*, 69 F.2d 809 (2d Cir. 1934).
[25] *Gregory v. Helvering*, 293 U.S. 465 (1935).

had ultimately won her case, corporations could easily make noncash distributions to their shareholders without a tax on the corporation and the shareholder by transferring property into a controlled corporation and distributing the stock in the controlled corporation to the parent's shareholders. Moreover, although Mrs. Gregory was not successful in her scheme, a slight variation in the facts could yield a favorable result for the taxpayer. For example, what if the assets transferred to the subsidiary were not highly liquid? Or, what if Mrs. Gregory had retained the distributed stock for a year or more? Or, what if the shareholder purchased a minor interest in a corporation under a plan whereby that stock was to be redeemed using the stock of a subsidiary corporation?

The major point of the previous discussion is that the spin-off and split-off rules when *Gregory* was decided were ripe for exploitation; moreover, the Supreme Court's decision would prevent abuses only in the most extreme cases. Thus, more rigorous tests were necessarily added to the Internal Revenue Code, as will be discussed in the following chapter.

However, even with the current more rigorous standards, corporations and shareholders have been able to use the spin-off and split-off techniques to achieve significant tax deferrals and savings. For example, DuPont acquired control of Conoco Corporation in a nontaxable reorganization and then used appreciated Conoco stock to redeem DuPont stock in the form of a split-off (i.e., DuPont offered to its shareholders Conoco shares in exchange for DuPont shares). In the final analyses, DuPont used its appreciated property (Conoco stock) to buy its own stock, and neither DuPont nor its former shareholders recognized taxable income. In other cases, a parent corporation that owned 100 percent of the subsidiary stock caused the subsidiary to issue (up to 20 percent) new stock to the public for cash, which was used to pay a nontaxable dividend to the parent (not taxable because of the corporate dividend received deduction) and then the subsidiary was spun off to the parents' shareholders.[26] Also, nontaxable results have been obtained from the subsidiary borrowing to

---

[26]To understand the benefits of the latter scheme, compare what was actually done to the result of the parent selling 20 percent of its subsidiary stock to the public and then distributing the remaining stock.

make nontaxable distributions to the parent before the parent spun off the subsidiary with its new debt.

In summary, the spin-off and split-off rules, when applied in the appropriate circumstances, neutralize the tax effects of transactions motivated by nontax business considerations. In some situations, the transactions would have been undertaken, regardless of the tax consequences; nevertheless, if the same economic results can be achieved without the tax, the client expects his tax professionals to assure the tax benefits are forthcoming.

Doing the Numbers

Sale of an Interest

Example: E and F each contribute $100 to E&F Inc. The corporation used $100 to purchase operating assets and $100 to form a subsidiary, S Inc., which used the cash to purchase operating assets for another business. E&F Inc. had $200 in earnings & profits when the value of S Inc. increased to $300, and the value of E&F Inc., exclusive of the value of the S subsidiary was $500, and S Inc. basis in its assets was $100. E and F decided to part ways. At that point, E and F had invested $200 in a corporation with a value of $800, for a net increase in value of $600. The balance sheet before the split is presented in the following table.

	Basis	Value	Unrealized Gain
E&F Inc.			
Operating assets	$300	$500	$200
Investment in Sub Inc.	$100	$300	$200
Total	$400	$800	$400
Shareholder equity			
E capital stock	$100	$400	$300
F capital stock	$100	$400	$300
Earnings and profit	$200		
Total	$400	$800	$400

Either shareholder could purchase the other shareholders E&F stock for its fair market value, and the seller would have a $300 gain, the buyer would have a basis in the newly purchased shares equal to what he or she paid, but E&F would be unaffected by the change in the shareholder's holdings: E&F would have no taxable gain or loss and its basis in assets would be unchanged. Assuming E purchased F's interest for $400, F would have a realized gain of $300 ($400 − $100), E would have 100 percent of the stock with a value of $800 and his basis in the stock would be $500 ($100 + $400); thus, E would have an unrealized gain of $800 − $500 = $300, and E&F Inc. would have a $400 ($800 − $400) unrealized gain. Therefore, the total realized and unrealized gain from the $400 increase, $200 income from operations in the value of E&F Inc. would be $1,400, which is greater than twice the corporation's realized and unrealized income (2 × [$800 − $200]) = $1,200, which is the correct result under a system of double taxation of corporate income. The extra $200 in taxable income generated by the corporation is due to the appreciation in the value of Sub Inc. assets. The appreciation in the Sub Inc. assets created $100 gain for F from the sale of the E&F stock, it will create $200 gain for Sub Inc. when it sells its assets and $200 gain when E&F Inc. sells its Sub Inc. stock, and it created a $100 gain for E when he sells his E&F stock.

Distribute Sub, §355	E&F	E	F	Sub	Total
Distribute Sub, §355					
Fair market value	$800	$800	$400	$300	
Basis in asset	$ (400)	$ (500)	$ (100)	$ 100)	
Deferred gain	$400	$300		$200	$900
Recognized gain			$300		$300
E&F after-tax income	$200				$200
Total income					$1,400

As can be seen below, a section 355 distribution can eliminate the triple taxation of the $200 unrealized appreciation in Sub Inc. assets.

Spin-Off

Before addressing the very detailed requirements of section 355, the effects of satisfying those requirements are illustrated. An example of a spin-off (i.e., the shareholders in the parent receive the subsidiary stock in a distribution in proportion to their stock in the parent) is used to illustrate the application of section 355 and its effects on all the relevant parties.

Example: E and F each contribute $100 to E&F Inc. The corporation used $100 to purchase operating assets and $100 to form a subsidiary, S Inc., which used the cash to purchase operating assets for another business. Further assume the corporation had $200 in after-tax income (earnings & profits) and the value of S Inc. increased to $300. The value of E&F Inc. exclusive of the value of the S subsidiary increase to $500, and S Inc.'s basis in its assets was $100; for good business reasons, E&F decided to remove Sub from corporate ownership to their individual ownership by distributing the Sub stock in proportion to their interests in the parent corporation. The balance sheet before the split is presented in the following table.

	Basis	Value	Unrealized Gain
E&F Inc.			
Operating assets	$300	$500	$200
Investment in Sub Inc.	$100	$300	$200
Total	$400	$800	$400
Shareholder equity			
E capital stock	$100	$400	$300
F capital stock	$100	$400	$300
Earnings and profits	$200		
Total	$400	$800	$600

Assuming all of the requirements for a nontaxable spin-off are satisfied, E and F will each have stock in the two corporations after the distribution. Their original bases in the parent stock must be allocated between the parent corporation and the subsidiary. The allocation is based on the relative fair market values of the stock.[27] Because the parent (without the

---

[27]Reg. §1. 358-2(a)(2)(iv).

subsidiary) and the subsidiary are of equal value, E's $100 basis in the E&F Inc. stock must be allocated between the E&F Inc. stock and the Sub stock:

$$\$100 \times \$500/\$800 = \$62.50 \text{ basis in E\&F Inc., and}$$
$$\$100 \times \$300/\$800 = \$37.50 \text{ basis in Sub.}$$

The calculations would be the same for F, since his basis in the E&F stock is the same as E's basis and the shareholders receive stock in Sub of equal value.

Under the general rules of section 311, E&F realized a gain of ($300 − $100) = $200 from the distribution. This gain is not recognized because the distribution qualified for section 355.[28]

Distribute Sub, §355 Parent's basis = shareholder's Basis	E&F	E	F	Sub	Total
Distribute Sub §355					
Fair market value	$500	$400	$400	$300	
Basis in asset	$300	$ (100)	$ (100)	$ (100)	
Deferred income	$200	$300	$300	$200	$1,000
E&F after-tax income	$200				$200
					$1,200

Thus, the original investors contributed $200 to the corporation capital, the assets increased in value to $800, an increase of $800 − $200 = $600. As demonstrated above, the section 355 distribution produced $1,200 in taxable income (current and deferred), whereas a sale of an interest result resulted in ultimate taxable income of $1,400. In effect, the section 355 distribution resulted in the avoidance of a second tax on the corporation's earnings and profits.

---

[28]Section 355(c)(1).

Spin-Off with Boot

Example: The facts are same as the previous example, except the Sub stock was distributed equally to E&F and, in addition, each shareholder received $25 cash. Thus, each shareholder received assets with a value of ½ ($300) + $25 = $175.

The $25 each shareholder received is taxed as a dividend out of the corporation's $200 earnings and profits.[29] This is true because each shareholder received $25 cash and gave up nothing in return. Each shareholder must allocate his or her basis in the E&F stock between E&F and the Sub stock based on relative fair market value, as computed above: The corporation does not recognize gain, as discussed above. However, if the boot had been property other than cash, the corporation would be required to recognize gain equal to the excess of the value of the boot property over the parent's basis.[30]

Distribute Sub, §355 Parent's basis = shareholder's basis	E&F	E	F	Sub	Total
Distribute Sub + $50, §355					
Fair market value	$450	$375*	$375*	$300	
Basis in asset	$ (150)	$ (100)	$ (100)	$ (200)	
Deferred income	$300	$275	$275	$100	$950
Recognized income		$25	$25		$50
E&F after-tax income	$200				$200
					$1,200

* $400 − $25 = $375

Split-Off with Boot

Example: E and F each contribute $200 to E&F Inc. The corporation used $300 to purchase operating assets and $100 to form a subsidiary, S Inc., which used the cash to purchase operating assets for another business. Further assume that when the value of S Inc. was $300 and the value

---

[29]Sections 358(c) and 356(a).
[30]Section 355(c)(2).

of E&F Inc. exclusive of the value of the S subsidiary was $500, and S Inc. basis in its assets was $100. E and F decided to part ways: F surrendered his E&F stock and received the Sub Inc. stock and $100 cash, under conditions in which all of the requirements of section 355 are satisfied.

	Basis	Value	Unrealized Gain
E&F Inc. from beginning			
Operating assets	$300	$500	$200
Investment in Sub Inc.	$100	$300	$200
Total	$400	$800	$400
Shareholder equity			
E	$200	$400	$200
F	$200	$400	$200
Total	$400	$800	$400

F has a realized gain of $200, equal to the amount realized ($300 value of Sub. Inc. stock + $100 cash), less F's basis in the E&F stock ($200). F's realized gain is recognized, but not more than the $100 cash (boot) received.[31] F's basis in the Sub stock is equal to his basis in the E&F stock less, the boot received, and plus the gain recognized,[32] $200 − $100 + $100 = $200. Thus, F has a deferred gain of $300 − $200 = $100 from the Sub stock received and a current gain of $100. The character (capital gain or dividend) of the $100 gain, under section 356(b), is determined by applying the stock redemption rules of section 302.[33] Assuming F's redemption resulted in a complete termination of his interest in E&F, under section 302(b)(3), F would report a capital gain; otherwise, if, for example, F remained an employee of E&F, the requirements for a complete termination of an interest would not be deemed satisfied and, therefore, the $100 would be taxed as a dividend.

As illustrated in the following paragraph, F's currently taxed $100 gain could have been deferred by E&F transferring $100 cash to the

---

[31]Section 356(b).

[32]Section 358(a).

[33]Section 356(a)(2); *Commissioner v. Clark*, 489 U.S. 726 (1989).

subsidiary, so that the value of the Sub stock would be $400, the value of F's interest in E&F; or, E&F could have paid $100 of F's liabilities.[34]

Split-Off, Equalizing Values but Avoiding Boot

The departing shareholder in a split-off expects to receive the stock in a subsidiary with a value equal to the value of his or her interest in the distributing corporation. The values may not initially equate; thus, it is necessary to either trim or augment the assets of the subsidiary. Continuing the previous example before E&F had any taxable income and assuming all of the requirements for section 355 are satisfied, F accepts all of the Sub stock in redemption of his interest. However, the value of F's interest in the parent is $400, but the value of the Sub Inc. stock is $300. To equalize values, E&F could transfer $100 cash to the Sub. Neither E&F nor F would be required to recognize gain, and F's basis in the Sub stock distributed would be, $200, the same as his basis in E&F. E&F would have remaining assets with a basis of $200 (original basis $400 − $100 basis in S less $100 transferred to S) and a value of $400 and, therefore, would have a deferred (unrealized) gain. F would also have an unrealized gain of $200. The results of the application of section 355 to the distribution in redemption of F's stock are summarized in the following table.

Distribute Sub, §355 Parent's basis = shareholder's basis	E&F	E	F	Sub	Total
Distribute Sub + $100, §355					
Fair market value	$400	$400	$400	$400	
Basis in asset	$ (200)	$ (200)	$ (200)	$ (200)	
Deferred income	$200	$200	$200	$200	$800

[34]As will be discussed later in these materials, the cash transfers or paying liabilities may be evidence of a "device." See. Rev. Rul. 83-114, 1983-2 C.B. 66. E&F could transfer the 15 percent of the F stock to a new corporation in exchange for its stock (a section 351 transfer), as was in *Dunn's Trust*, 86 T.C. 745. See, J.L. Cummings. February, 2009. "New Temporary Regulations Cool Off the Hot Stock Rule for Divisive Transactions," *Journal of Taxation* 110, no. 2, p. 69.

CHAPTER 2

General Requirements for a Tax-Free Spin-Off or Split-Off

Statutory and Judicial Requirements

In General

This chapter introduces the requirements for a nontaxable spin-off or split-off in general terms. Subsequent chapters will further analyze the section 355 requirements.

Section 355 contains several requirements intended to prevent possible abuses similar to what was attempted by Mrs. Gregory and other taxpayers. Some of the requirements are objective, and others require a judgment call after considering all the facts and circumstances evaluated in light of the purpose of the law.

According to section 355, the underlying regulations, and court decisions, the following requirements must be satisfied for the spin-off or split-off to be nontaxable.

1. There must be a business purpose for the distribution to the shareholders.[1]
2. The distribution must not be principally used as a "device" to distribute the corporation's earnings and profits to its shareholders.[2]

---

[1] *Gregory v. Helvering*, 293 U.S. 465 (1935).
[2] Section 355(a)(1)(B).

3. There must be a continuity of ownership by shareholders in the distributing corporation and the corporation whose stock is distributed (the controlled corporation).[3]

4. A corporation must distribute to its shareholders a controlling (80 percent) interest in another corporation.[4]

5. The distributing and the controlled corporations must be engaged in the active conduct of a trade or business immediately after the distribution.[5]

6. The trade or businesses must have been actively conducted for at least 5 years prior to the distribution.[6]

7. The trade or business must not have been acquired by purchase within 5 years before the distribution.[7]

8. A corporate shareholder cannot have acquired control of the distributing corporation during the 5 years ending on the date of its distribution;[8]

9. A corporation making a distribution of purchased stock must have owned the stock at least five years at the time of the distribution.[9]

Additional requirements must be satisfied in specific circumstances that are discussed later.

The distribution of control of the corporation requirement makes clear that a substantial change in the corporate structure must occur. The active conduct of a trade or business requirement distinguishes the events from cases such as Mrs. Gregory's corporation distributing investment assets. Requiring the trade or business to have been conducted by the corporation for 5 years before the distribution prevents abuses such as the distributing corporation acquiring control of another corporation and immediately distributing the newly purchased stock. There must be a corporate business purpose for the distribution, rather than merely a means to achieve a tax savings for the shareholder or the corporation. The device

---

[3]Section 355(c).
[4]Section 355(a)(1)(D).
[5]Section 355(b).
[6]Section 355(b)(2).
[7]Section 355(b)(2)(B).
[8]Section 355(b)(2)(D).
[9]Section 355(a)(3)(B).

test allows the *Internal Revenue Service* (IRS) and the courts to look at the facts and circumstances to determine whether the transactions are essentially equivalent to an ordinary dividend. Finally, the continuity of interest requirement carries out the concept of a reshuffling of ownership in commonly owned and operated businesses.

Distribution of Control

Whether the control requirement is satisfied can be objectively determined. Immediately before the distribution, the distributing corporation must "control" the corporation whose stock is being distributed, and, as a result of the distribution, the distributing corporation's shareholders must control the corporation whose stock is distributed. *Control* is defined in section 368(c) as "ownership of stock possessing 80 percent of the total combined voting power of all the classes of stock entitled to vote and at least 80 percent of the total number of shares of all other classes of stock of the corporation."[10]

If the required 80 percent of the stock is distributed but some of the stock is retained by the distributing corporation, an additional requirement must be satisfied: Tax avoidance cannot be a principal purpose of the retention.[11] Thus, assume that P distributed 85 percent of the stock in its subsidiary, but sold the 15 percent of the stock at a gain that would be absorbed by a capital loss from other assets. The IRS would argue that a principal purpose of the plan was tax avoidance and, therefore, P would be required to recognize any gain from distributing the 85 percent of the stock (but not a loss), and its shareholders would be required to recognize dividend income from the failed spin-off.

Active Conduct of a Trade or Business

Both the distributing corporation and the controlled corporations whose stock is distributed must be actively engaged in a trade or business before and after the distribution.[12] The "active conduct of a trade or business"

---

[10]Section 355(a)(1)(D)(ii).

[11]Section 355(a)(1)(D).

[12]Section 355(b)(1).

requirement distinguishes the mere holding of an investment from conducting a business.

The trade or business requirement is clearly directed at Mrs. Gregory's situation—where the corporation whose stock was distributed engaged in no activity other than collecting dividends on stock it owned.[13] The spun-off corporation contained highly liquid assets, and the stock in the corporation that was spun off could be sold without interfering with the operations of the distributing corporation's business operations.[14]

Trade or Business Definition

Section 1.355-3(b)(2)(ii) defines a *trade or business* as "a specific group of activities [that] are being carried on by the corporation for the purpose of earning income or profit, and the activities included in such group include every operation that forms a part of, or a step in, the process of earning income or profit." In particular, "[s]uch group of activities ordinarily must include the collection of income and the payment of expenses."

The trade or business requirement has been extensively litigated to determine issues such as the distinction between a trade or business and a mere investment activity; whether an existing business can be vertically divided (e.g., based on physical location) or horizontally sliced (by business functions) into separate corporations that carry the same business history; and whether an existing business was expanded or a new business was created. Some of these issues are related to the 5-year requirement.

The 5-Year Requirement

The distributing corporation and the corporation whose stock is being distributed must be actively conducting a trade or business which it has operated for at least 5 years at the time of the distribution.[15] This requirement prevents the corporation from accumulating cash, purchasing stock in another corporation to distribute to the acquiring corporation's

---

[13]See W.L. John. 1972. "Active Conduct" Distinguished from "Conduct" of a Rental Real Estate Business *Active,* 25 Tax Lawyer 317.

[14]Reg. §1.355-2(d)(2)(iv)(c).

[15]Section 355(b)(1) and (2).

shareholders. Furthermore, a trade or business conducted by the distributing and controlled corporations must not have been acquired in a taxable transaction (e.g., by purchase) during the 5-year period preceding the distribution. The type of activity the 5-year requirement prevents is illustrated in the following example:[16]

> Example: Individual B owns 100 percent of the stock in D Corporation, which has actively conducted a trade or business for 5 years. D Corporation has excess cash and B desires to acquire business C, a proprietorship. B directs D Corporation to purchase all of the business C assets, transfer them to a newly formed C Corporation, and distribute the C stock to her. The spin-off will be taxable because the business purchased had not been actively conducted by D Corporation for 5 years at the time of the distribution.

In the above example, B was using D Corporation's assets to acquire an unincorporated business for B, which is far different than dividing an existing corporation. However, if the C business were incorporated before D Corporation acquired the stock and the acquisition was a nontaxable transaction [e.g., a section 368(a)(1)(B) reorganization], the C Corporation business history would survive the acquisition. For example, if C Corporation had conducted its trade or business for 3 years prior to the nontaxable reorganization with D Corporation, the 5-year test will be satisfied once C Corporation had continued the business for 2 years after D Corporation acquired control of C Corporation.[17]

The 5-Year Requirement and "Hot Stock"

Section 355 comes into vogue when a corporation distributes at least 80 percent of the outstanding stock in another corporation. However, for the distribution to be totally nontaxable, none of the stock distributed can have been acquired by purchase within 5 years of the distribution.

------

[16]See H. Report No. 2543 (1954) at p. 37.
[17]See *W.E. Gabriel Fabrication Co.,* 42 T.C. 545 (1964); S. Rept. No. 1622, to accompany H.R. 8300 (Pub. L. No. 591), 83d Cong., 2d Sess. 50-51 (1954).

Example: P Corporation purchased 85 percent of all of the T Corporation stock for cash in 2018. In 2022, in transactions separate from the 2018 purchase, P purchased the remaining 15 percent of the T stock. T had been actively conducting a trade or business in all of its years. In 2024, P distributed all of the T stock to the P shareholders. The control requirement was satisfied because P acquired at least 80 percent of the stock in a nontaxable transaction more than 5 years before the distribution and distributed at least 80 percent of the T stock to the P shareholders.

It should be noted that in the above example, the 15 percent of the stock purchased in 2022 and distributed did not satisfy the 5-year test and, therefore, the distribution of the value of that stock is taxable as boot received: The realized gain will be taxable to the shareholder, but the taxable gain cannot exceed the value of the boot.[18] Also, the distributing corporation must recognize any realized gain from the distribution of the disqualified (15 percent) stock.[19] The exception to this rule is that if P purchased the final 15 percent of the stock from another member of an affiliated group under the consolidated return rules, the additional 15 percent is not boot.[20]

Note: In the above example, if P purchased 85 percent of the T stock in 2020 and distributed it in 2024, the five years of ownership requirement would not be satisfied and thus the distribution would be taxable to P and the P shareholders

Corporate Business Purpose for the Distribution

The primary purpose of Mrs. Gregory's maneuvers was to enable her to receive direct ownership of the corporation's investment assets that she could convert to cash in a tax-efficient manner. The transfer of the assets and the liquidation of the transferee corporation did not serve a business purpose of the distributing corporation. As Judge Learned Hand observed, Congress enacted the spin-off rules so that the tax laws would

---

[18]Reg. §1.355-2(g)(1) and section 356(a).
[19]Section 361(b).
[20]Section 255(b)(3)(B).

be neutral in regard to reorganizing corporations and their ownership that were compelled by business considerations,[21] which was lacking in Mrs. Gregory's case. The corporate business purpose was later made an explicit requirement in Reg. §1.355-2(b). What constitutes a corporate business purpose will be the subject of Chapter 3 in these materials.

Not Used Principally as a Device

The *device* referred to in the Code is the shifting of income between and among taxpayers and the recharacterization (from ordinary to capital gain) of income.[22] The initial tax benefit of a spin-off or a split-off is that the shareholder is able to receive assets from the corporation without recognizing income from the distribution. Instead of recognizing income, the shareholder allocates some of his or her basis in the distributing corporation stock to the distributed stock based on their relative fair market values.[23]

> Example: B, an individual, owns stock in P Corporation with a basis of $90 and $240 fair market value, when the corporation distributes stock in a subsidiary, S Corporation, with a fair market value of $80. After the distribution the fair market value of B's P stock decreases to ($240 − $80) = $160. Assuming the distribution met all of requirements for a nontaxable section 355 distribution, B is not taxed on the distribution; his basis in the S stock is $90 × $80/($160 + $80) = $30, and his basis in the P stock is $90 × $160/($160 + $80) = $60.

The distribution not only deferred income, it shifted income from the disposition of P stock to the disposition of S stock through the allocation the basis in the stock and recharacterized the ultimate income from ordinary dividend when the stock was received as a distribution to capital gain when the stock is sold. Thus, the distribution must not be "principally a device"—that is enabled by section 355—for deferring, shifting, and recharacterizing (from ordinary to capital gain) income.[24] If the spin-off

---

[21]69 F.2d 809 (1934), at 811.

[22]See Reg. §1.355-2(d)(1).

[23]Section 358(b).

[24]See Reg. §1.355-2(d)(1).

or split-off is "principally" used to defer, shift, and recharacterize income, these objectives will not be achieved. On the other hand, if these are not the principal objectives of the transactions, but rather are a byproduct of distributing the stock to carryout a business purpose, these benefits will be granted. Therefore, to justify obtaining the obvious tax benefits, the taxpayer must establish one or more business purposes as the principal reason for the transactions.

As discussed above, the policy justification for section 355 is to neutralize the tax laws in regard to business decisions that necessitate a distribution of the stock in a controlled corporation. The neutrality works both ways; that is, the tax laws are not neutral if they interfere with a valid business reason to do a certain thing, and the laws are not neutral if the tax benefits are the reason for doing something that is not justified on the merits of its nontax business benefits. However, the taxpayer is not required to prove that the decision would not be made if the distribution were taxed. Rather, the taxpayer must merely convince the IRS that the business reasons dominate the decision-making process.

The regulations list and discuss a number of factors that are evidence of a "device" and evidence indicating the distribution was not a "device," as will be discussed in Chapter 4. The trier of the facts must balance these factors and reach a conclusion whether the distribution was used principally as a "device" for achieving the tax benefits made available by section 355.

Continuity of Interest

The continuity requirement is a general requirement for a corporate reorganization and is used as a means of distinguishing a reorganization from a sale. It requires that a substantial proportion of the investors in the distributing corporation must continue to maintain an ownership interest in the distributing and controlled corporation's stock. The purpose of the continuity of interest requirement is to distinguish a corporate division from a sale of stock.[25] As will be further discussed in Chapter 6, the complications in evaluating this requirement occur when shareholders acquire or dispose of their stock soon after the distributions.

---

[25]Reg. §1.355-2(c)(1); Rev. Rul. 79-273, 1979-2 C.B. 125.

CHAPTER 3

Corporate Business Purpose

In General

The economic benefit from a spin-off or split-off is that a shareholder is able to extract appreciated assets from the corporation without the current recognition of taxable income.[1] Under the general rules of taxation, both the shareholder[2] and the corporation[3] would have taxable income from moving corporate assets to the shareholder. The justification for this exception to the general rules is that certain transactions that make "good business sense" will not occur (or are less likely to occur) if the events create a current tax liability, as in cases such as *Rockefeller*[4] (a spin-off to facilitate compliance with regulatory authority) or *Gabriel Fabrication*[5] (a split-off because of managerial disputes by owners). To qualify for these extraordinary benefits of section 355, corporation management must present to the Internal Revenue Service (IRS) compelling evidence that the distribution of the stock to the shareholders serves a significant corporate business purpose. In situations where it is necessary to transfer assets to a newly formed corporation before the distribution of the stock, the creation of the corporation is easily defended as serving a corporate purpose, for example, limiting its liability. But the very act of shifting

---

[1]The IRS will issue a letter ruling on a significant issue under Reg. 1.355-2(b) pertaining to business purpose if the issue is a legal issue and is not inherently factual in nature. Rev. Proc. 2020-3, 3.01(62), 2020-1 I.R.B. 131. The IRS had stopped issuing any letter rulings on business purpose under Code Sec. 355 in 2003. See Rev. Proc. 2003-48, 2003-2 C.B. 86.

[2]Section 301.

[3]Section 311.

[4]*Rockefeller v. United States*, 257 U.S. 176 (1921), discussed in Chapter 1.

[5]*W.E. Gabriel Fabrication Co.,* 42 T.C. 545 (1964), also discussed in Chapter 1.

assets, liabilities, and business activity to a new corporation limits the liability of the transferor. The difficulty under the tax law is justifying the distribution of the stock as serving a corporate business purpose.

The spin-off may serve a shareholder nontax purpose as well as a corporate business purpose, and as a result, the shareholders will enjoy double benefits from a spin-off. For example, a spin-off of risky assets may enhance the value of the stock (serving a shareholder purpose) and thereby enhance the distributing corporation's ability to raise capital (a corporate business purpose). However, the fact that the distribution is made to serve a shareholder personal purpose but was not tax motivated is not justification for exempting the spin-off. A corporate business purpose must be served by the distribution. Thus, in *Rafferty v. Commissioner*,[6] the closely held corporation attempted to spin off some of its operations into a separate corporation to facilitate the major shareholder's estate planning. The major shareholder's dominant goal was to divide the corporation so that he could gift his shares in each corporation to his children according to the needs and abilities of each child. The major shareholder considered some of the children incapable of operating one portion of the business, and therefore, these children would receive stock in the business that required less management ability. The court considered the plan to be based solely on the shareholder's personal estate planning objectives, rather than to serve a business purpose of the corporation; therefore, the spin-off was taxable. On the other hand, in Revenue Ruling 2003-52,[7] the split-off had personal family planning benefits, but the corporate business purpose (more efficient business operations) was deemed the primary purpose for a split-off.

In short, if the spin-off or split-off serves a valid business purpose, but the shareholders realize tax benefits as a result, the fact of these tax benefits will not cause a denial of the tax benefits. Nevertheless, the more compelling the business purpose for the spin-off or split-off, the more likely the taxpayer will receive the tax benefits.

---

[6]452 F.2d 767 (1st Cir. 1971), *aff'g* 55 T.C. 490 (1970).
[7]2003-1 C.B. 960.

The Regulations

The regulations provide nine examples of when the business purpose requirement for the distribution is satisfied and when it is not satisfied. These examples illustrate that to justify the distribution as business purpose, the corporation must be prepared to demonstrate that alternatives to satisfy the business purpose that do not require a distribution of stock are neither impractical of unduly expensive.[8]

Spin-Off to Satisfy Regulators Justifies a Spin-Off

In the first example,[9] the corporate business purpose requirement was satisfied because the corporation was required by regulators to divest a division of the business, which was accomplished as a spin-off. The regulators required that not only was it necessary to place the business in a separate corporation, it was necessary for the distributing corporation to terminate its ownership of the business.

More Efficient Operations Justifies a Split-Off

In the second example,[10] the corporation was equally owned by two shareholders, and the corporation conducted two businesses of equal value. Each shareholder was interested in only one of the businesses, and the two businesses could be better operated if one shareholder devoted all of his or her time to one of the businesses and the other shareholder devoted his or her time to the other business. The more efficient operations and resulting enhanced values satisfied the business purpose requirement for the business separation and distribution.

---

[8]Reg. §1.355-2(b)(3).
[9]Reg. §1.355-2(d)(4), Example 1.
[10]Reg. §1.355-2(d)(4), Example 2.

Reduction in Risk

The third example[11] is of a corporation that manufactures toys and candy. The toy business was transferred to a controlled corporation to avoid the possibility of tort claims endangering the candy business assets. Then the toy business stock was distributed to the shareholders of the original corporation. The potential liability from the toy business could be limited by the mere transfer of the toy business assets to the new corporation; thus, the distribution of the stock was not necessary to serve the professed purpose of the transaction and thus the spin-off was taxable.

Regulated Prices

The fourth example[12] is another case of a spin-off undertaken because of business regulations. Two businesses were lodged in one corporation, one business was subject to state regulations that affected the prices that could be charged customers of the nonregulated business. The pricing constraints on the nonregulated business could be eliminated by creating a new corporation, transferring the nonregulated business to the new corporation in exchange for stock. But the original corporation also distributed to its shareholder the stock in the new corporation. Because the distribution of the stock was not necessary to the original business purpose, avoiding pricing restrictions, the transaction was a taxable spin-off.

The fifth example[13] is the same as the fourth, except that the pricing regulations applied to the parent and subsidiary on a consolidated basis, but would not apply to the subsidiary business if its stock were not owned by the parent. Therefore, following the transfer of the assets to the subsidiary, the parent distributed to its shareholders the subsidiary stock. The distribution satisfied a corporate purpose, and therefore, the distribution could be a nontaxable spin-off.

---

[11]Reg. §1.355-2(d)(4), Example 3. It should be noted that if the candy business were a subsidiary of the corporation with the toy business, the spin-off would prevent the toy business creditors access to the candy business assets.

[12]Reg. §1.355-2(d)(4), Example 4.

[13]Reg. §1.355-2(d)(4), Example 5.

To Make an S Corporation Election and Thereby Reduce Federal Income Taxes

The sixth example[14] has two variations. In the first, a parent corporation owns 100 percent of the subsidiary's stock. The parent corporation distributed the stock to its shareholder. The purpose of the distribution was to enable the corporation whose stock was distributed to make an S corporation election and thereby reduce the tax on the corporation's income. According to the regulation, reducing the federal corporate tax is not a valid corporate purpose and, therefore, the spin-off was taxable. In the second variation of an S election, the corporation operated two divisions; therefore, it was necessary to create a new corporation by transferring assets for stock and then distributing the stock to original corporation's shareholders so that the corporation could elect to be an S corporation. Again, this was not a valid corporate purpose, and therefore, the spin-off was taxable.

To Make an S Corporation Election and Reduce State Income Taxes

The seventh example[15] is another play on spin-off so as to qualify for an S election. But in this example, the S election would reduce state taxes as well as federal taxes, but the election would result in a much greater reduction in federal income taxes. The state tax savings was not sufficient to create a valid business purpose to justify a nontaxable spin-off.

The lesson from Examples 6 and 7 in the regulations is that saving federal income tax is not a valid business purpose justifying the distribution. Moreover, although saving state taxes may be a valid business purpose, to grant federal tax benefit so that the corporation may gain state tax benefits may be too much of a good thing.

To Facilitate Employee Stock Ownership

In the final example[16] in the regulations, the corporation conducts two businesses and would like to enable an employee in one division to attain

---

[14] Reg. §1.355-2(d)(4), Example 6.

[15] Reg. §1.355-2(d)(4), Example 7.

[16] Reg. §1.355-2(b)(5), Example 8.

an equity interest in only the business the employee serves. Therefore, a new corporation was created, and the assets of one of the businesses were transferred in exchange for all of the new corporation's stock. It was necessary to distribute the stock of the new corporation to the employee so that the employee could participate only in the value he or she created. The business purpose for the distribution was valid.

Other IRS Guidance

In General

In a series of revenue procedures, the IRS has provided additional guidance as to what is considered a sufficiently compelling business purpose to justify not taxing the spin-off or split-off. As discussed above, the corporation must demonstrate to the IRS that the purported purposes are substantial and germane to the business. For example, an attempt to justify the spin-off to enable the employee to own stock in the businesses, he or she serves requires that the corporation convince the Service that the employee can see the relationship between his or her performance and the value of the stock. Moreover, the corporation must demonstrate that the business purpose cannot be achieved through an alternative nontaxable transaction that is neither impractical nor unduly expensive.

In Revenue Procedure 96-30,[17] the Service discussed the following possible (illustrative but not exhaustive) business purposes that justify not taxing the distribution of the stock:

1. To provide an equity interest to employees
2. To facilitate a stock offering
3. To facilitate borrowing
4. To resolve management problems ("Fit and focus")
5. To create cost savings
6. To resolve problems of competing with the corporation's customers or suppliers
7. To facilitate a tax-free acquisition of the distributing corporation

---

[17] 1996-1 C.B. 686.

8. To facilitate a tax-free acquisition of another corporation by the distributing or controlled corporation
9. To protect business from risk associated with another business operated by the distributing corporation.

Provide an Equity Interest for Key Employees

The employee's stock ownership in his or her corporate employer is generally considered to provide an incentive for the employee to provide more diligent services and loyalty to the corporation. The incentive is greatest when the stock is in a corporation that does not contain businesses that are unaffected by the employee's performance. Also, the greater the employee's relative ownership, the greater the incentive to perform well. Of course, there are other ways to reward employees, such as cash bonuses. But unlike cash, the stock represents a more permanent relationship between the employer and the corporation's employees. However, the employee's ownership can be so small, and the entity's earnings are subject to many vagaries that in reality owning stock will not serve as a meaningful incentive for the employee. Therefore, to justify the nontaxable spin-off, the corporation must intend that the employees will have a meaningful interest in the corporation. If the spin-off is in a publicly held corporation, it is unlikely that the employee will obtain a meaningful interest, unlike in the case of closely held corporations.

More specifically, Revenue Procedure 96-30[18] required the taxpayer to present evidence and representations as to the following:

1. Why the employee or employees were important to the business
2. Why the employee or employees required an equity interest of the type and amount proposed
3. That the employee or employees will receive a "significant amount of stock" within 1 year of the distribution
4. An alternative nontaxable approach to accomplish the objective was not practical or was unduly expensive (e.g., transfer to a partnership or an LLC).

---

[18]Rev. Proc. 96-30, Appendix A, §2.01(1).

In an example in the proposed regulations, individual A owned 100 percent of P Corporation stock and P owned 100 percent of C Corporation stock. Individual B was an employee who was critical to the success of P Corporation and demanded an ownership interest in P. However, B could not afford to purchase the P stock because its value was inflated by the value of the C stock. Therefore, C Corporation stock was spun off to individual A, and A sold some of his P stock to B. The business purpose for the spin-off was satisfied. However, in light of the fact that the business purpose could have been satisfied by P issuing new shares to B (rather than to A), an alternative that would also not be taxable event,[19] the transactions may be considered a device for A to receive capital gains treatment from the sale of his stock.[20]

Planned Stock Offering

When the corporation has definite plans for a stock offering to finance capital expenditures, retire debt, or other business needs, separating the businesses may enable the corporation to raise more capital per share issued. A spin-off may be a means of separating the debt from one line of business from another trade or business that is in need of equity financing from the public.[21] Also, when the corporation has more than one line of business and the price to earnings ratios for the businesses differ, if the capital is needed for the business that can justify the higher price ratio, separating the lower price earnings ratio business into a separate corporation and distributing the stock of that business will increase the offering price of the stock in the business that needs the funds.[22]

New Debt

A spin-off can be justified on the basis that the separation will enable the corporation to borrow significantly more money or to borrow on better

---

[19]Reg. §1.355-2(b)(3).

[20]See Prop. Reg. §1.355-2(d)(4), Example 1.

[21]See, e.g., Rev. Rul. 82-13, 1982-2 C.B. 83.

[22]Rev. Rul. 2004-23, IRB 2004-11.

terms.[23] For example, a corporation that is in a risky business in need a loan for its lower risk business can negotiate for better debt terms if the lower risk business is placed in a separate corporation and that corporation borrows the funds. Distributing the stock of the low-risk business to the parent's shareholders will reduce its possible entanglements with the riskier operations. However, the spin-off may be prompted by a desire to reduce shareholder's exposure to risk. For example, if the high-risk business were lodged in the parent, and the parent borrows, all of the corporate assets may be at risk of default. Placing the low-risk assets in a subsidiary corporation will not reduce the exposure to creditors because the subsidiary would still be the parent's asset, but distributing the subsidiary stock will eliminate the creditor's access to those assets, which would serve a corporate and shareholder purpose.

Fit and Focus

Combined or integrated operations often create synergy in the form of cost reductions. However, the combination may result in "negative synergy," in that the management may wish to concentrate on its core businesses without distractions from other operations. On the other hand, the noncore business may be starved for attention by management as resources are diverted to the core business. By separating the businesses, employees may devote their time and energy to the business he or she most interested in serving. Most frequently, fit and focus is the justification for a split-off, rather than for a spin-off.[24]

Cost Savings

Proving that cost savings will occur as a result of separating businesses may be difficult. Most often, combining businesses will facilitate cost reductions by eliminating duplicate administrative functions. However, in some circumstances, state taxes (other than income taxes) can be

---

[23]Rev. Proc. 96-30, Appendix A, §2.03(2). See, e.g., PLR 201135025; Rev. Rul. 2005-65 2005, 2005-2 C.B. 684.

[24]See, e.g., *Badanes v. Commissioner*, 39 T.C. 410 (1966); PLR 9843015; Rev. Rul. 2003-74, 2003-29 IRB 77.

reduced by separating the businesses operating into different states.[25] Also, insurance costs may be reduced by placing the riskier assets in a separate corporation.

Competition with Customers and Suppliers

A functionally integrated corporation that produces goods for sales to wholesalers and retailers may also make direct sales of goods to retail customers. By spinning off the business that competes with the corporation's competitors, the corporation's taint may be eliminated.[26]

Facilitate an Acquisition of the Distributing Corporation

Often, a corporation that is "in play" will have assets that are not attractive to the acquiror. The owners of the target corporation can make the acquisition more likely to happen by ridding itself of the unwanted assets. A spin-off may be a viable means of a nontaxable disposition of the unwanted assets, but presents another set of issues, as will be discussed later in these materials.[27]

Protection against Risk

Corporate assets may be subject to varying degrees of risk associated with other assets owned by the corporation and byproducts it sells. In many cases, the exposure can be reduced by transferring the assets to another corporation controlled by the transferor (the parent corporation). The problem with risk reduction as the reason for nontaxable spin-off is that the risk reduction is accomplished with the transfer of the assets to the controlled corporation and the distribution of the stock is unnecessary to accomplish the stated goal. However, if under state or federal law, in certain instances, the court can "pierce the corporate veil" and attribute the actions of the subsidiary to the parent and thus making the parent

---

[25]See, e.g., PLR 9804034, PLR 9742015.
[26]See, e.g., PLR 974003, PLR 200351005.
[27]See *Commissioner v. Morris Trust*, 367 F.2d 794 (1966).

liable, the spin-off may actually reduce the parent's risk and thus satisfy the business purpose requirement.[28]

Other Business Purposes

In *Rockefeller*,[29] discussed in Chapter 1, the corporate separation occurred before the tax laws were amended to accommodate the spin-off. The business reason for the corporation being divided into two corporations and distributing the stock was to simplify compliance with certain regulatory authorities. After the spin-off, only one of the corporations was subject to regulatory authority. However, simplifying regulatory compliance could be a valid business reason for dividing the business into two corporations, but that may not justify distributing the stock. The corporations could operate as a parent and subsidiary.

The split-off situation, as in *Gabriel*, where shareholders in conflict cause harm to the corporation seems, the easiest case to convince the Service that the distribution of the stock serves a business purpose.[30]

Finally, in communications with shareholders, corporate management will often justify the spin-off as enhancing "shareholder value," the idea being that the market value of the two corporations apart is greater than their value together, as though the combined businesses create negative synergy. But that claim, alone, will probably not satisfy the business purpose requirement. This is true because the enhancement of shareholder value is a shareholder purpose, rather than a corporate purpose. The corporation's success in achieving a nontaxable spin-off is more likely to occur if the corporation can relate the spin-off and value of the business to a planned stock issue, improved borrowing power, or employee compensation in the form of stock ownership.[31]

---

[28]See, J.R. Macey and J. Mitts. 2014. "Finding Order in the Morass: The Three Real Justifications for Piercing the Corporate Veil," *Cornell Law Review 100*, no. 99.

[29]*Rockefeller v. United States*, 257 U.S. 176 (1921).

[30]See, e.g., *Edmund P. Coady*, 33 T.C. 771, affd. 289 F.2d 49 (C.A. 6); *Badanes v. Commissioner*, 39 T.C. 410 (1962).

[31]See Re. Rul. 2004-23, IRB 2004-11.

Conclusions

The taxpayer must demonstrate a business purpose for the distribution of the stock. Even if the record shows the corporate owners did not consider the tax consequences of the distribution, in the absence of a corporate business purpose, the application of section 355 is not warranted.[32] This is true because if taxes were not a consideration, by definition, taxes were neutral to what was done and setting aside the general rules of taxation by applying section 355 is not warranted. The corporate business purpose, rather than a shareholder purpose, must be the driving force behind the actions.

---

[32]*Commissioner v. Wilson*, 353 F.2d 184 (9th Cir. 1965).

CHAPTER 4

Not Used Principally as a Device for Distributing Earnings and Profits

Introduction

In General

The previous chapter examined the corporation's required business purpose for the distribution to achieve section 355 benefits. This chapter looks at the factors that are considered in determining whether the distribution was made for a nonbusiness purpose; that is, "a device for the distribution of the earnings and profits of the distributing or controlled corporation."[1] The regulations elaborate on the concept of "device" without actually defining the term.

> Section 355 recognizes that a tax-free distribution of the stock of a controlled corporation presents a potential for tax avoidance by facilitating the avoidance of the dividend provisions of the Code through the subsequent sale or exchange of stock of one corporation and the **retention of the** stock **of another** corporation. A device can include a transaction that effects a recovery of basis.[2]

The author interprets this to mean that Treasury is aware that a distribution of property that is not taxed as a dividend, when combined with the basis rules, converts what would otherwise be a dividend received into sales proceeds that may ultimately be received at a later date. Thus, section

---

[1]Reg. §1.355-2(d)(1).
[2]Reg. §1.355-2(d)(1).

355 creates a deferral and possible change in the character of income. As related to the earlier discussion of the purpose of section 355, ideally, the corporation makes the distribution for a business purpose in a split-off or spin-off and the shareholder does not bear a tax burden, because, otherwise, the business decision would not be taken. Thus, the tax law must distinguish between distributions made principally for business purposes, with incidental tax benefits conferred on the shareholders, or distributions that were made principally for the tax benefits to the shareholder. An analysis of the facts and circumstances is necessary to assess the tax benefits relative to the business benefits presented and to reach a conclusion about whether the business purpose is primary.[3]

The Significance of the Sale of the Stock

In *Gregory*, Mrs. Gregory's sale of the distributed assets immediately after she received it raised issues about the substance of the transactions: When the steps were collapsed, the transfer of investment assets from her controlled corporation to another corporation she controlled, followed by the distribution and sale of the assets distributed to her, appeared to be an indirect means for her to obtain cash from her controlled corporation. But according to a double parenthetical statement in section 355(b), a sale of the stock does not necessarily decide the issue:

> (but the mere fact that subsequent to the distribution stock or securities in one or more of such corporations are sold or exchanged by all or some of the distributees (other than pursuant to an arrangement negotiated or agreed upon prior to such distribution) shall not be construed to mean that the transaction was used principally as such a device,…)

It seems apparent that at some point in time after the spin-off, in general, it would be expected that the shareholder will sell the distributed stock. A sale that is "negotiated or agreed upon prior to the distribution"[4] is clear evidence of a device. Absent the redistribution

---

[3]Section 355(a)(1)(B).

[4]Reg. §1.355-2(d)(2)(iii)(B).

negotiations, but a subsequent sale of the stock, the trier of the facts must decide whether the distribution plan was principally a device for distributing the corporation's earnings and profits.

On the other hand, the fact that the shareholder did not sell the stock does not mean the "not-as-a-device" test is satisfied. The mere ability to convert the stock to cash at any time the shareholder so chooses may be evidence of a device.[5] Thus, the regulations use a balancing of factors, as can be seen below.

The Regulations

The regulations provide a list of "device factors," conditions that are indicative of a device, and "non-device factors," conditions that indicate the distribution is not a device. In addition, the regulations provide what the author considers "safe harbors;" that is, where these conditions are present the inquiry is over.

Safe harbors	Device factors	Non-device factors
No earnings and profits	Pro rata distributions	Strong corporate business purpose
Stock redemptions (split-off)	Subsequent sale	Publicly traded
Pursuant to a reorganization	Nature of the assets	Corporate shareholders

Safe Harbors

The safe harbors are events that if they occurred, but the section 355 requirements were not satisfied, the shareholder would realize a capital gain or recovery of capital. Therefore, the shareholder would not need a "device" (e.g., a spin-off) to convert ordinary income into capital gain. If these circumstances exist, the device test is not an issue, but the transactions must still be tested for the other section requirements (i.e., business purpose, active conduct of a trade or business, continuity of interest).

---

[5]Reg. §1.355-2(d)(2)(iii)(C).

No Earnings and Profits.   Distributions from a corporation that does not have earnings and profits are not taxed as dividends.[6] The distribution is a recovery of basis in the stock, and once the basis has been recovered, any additional amount received is taxed as a capital gain.[7] Simply put, in the absence of earnings and profits, a distribution cannot be a device to distribute earnings and profits that do not exist. However, the regulations require an absence of earnings and profits in the distributing and the controlled corporation. Moreover, the regulations treat the existence of appreciated assets owned by the corporation making the distribution as a readily available source of earnings and profits as "actual earnings and profits."[8]

Stock Redemptions.   In a split-off, the shareholder gives up his or her shares in the distributing corporation in exchange for the distributed stock. If any of the section 355 requirements are not satisfied, the exchange is generally treated as a stock redemption under section 302. Assuming the requirements for capital gains under section 302 are satisfied, the redemption will be treated as a sale of stock. Because the split-off that does not satisfy the section 355 requirements would be taxed as a capital gain, generally, the split-off cannot be a device for achieving capital gains treatment; thus, the device test is not relevant[9] (see section "Pursuant to a Reorganization"). Section 303(a) redemptions to pay death taxes are also exempt from the device test.[10]

Pursuant to a Reorganization.   A spin-off is frequently a precursor to a corporate reorganization. For example, two corporations may desire to merge, but one of the corporations may have assets ill-suited for the combination. The wanted assets may be spun off prior to the reorganization and then the stock received in the spin-off may be exchange for stock in

---

[6]Sections 316(a) and 301(c).

[7]Section 243(a).

[8]Reg. §1.355-2(d)(5)(2)(ii)(C).

[9]Reg. §1.355-2(d)(5)(iv).

[10]Reg. §1.355-2(d)(5)(iii).

the acquiring corporation, or the unwanted assets may be spun off prior to a stock for stock exchange. A sale or other disposition of the stock following a section 355 distribution is generally indicative of a device. However, the regulations provide a safe harbor for exchanges of stock in a reorganization, provided the boot received is insubstantial.[11]

Device Factors

Pro rata Distributions.   A spin-off, by definition, requires a pro rata distribution of the stock. Therefore, it is not known why this would need to be separately stated as a condition to distinguish a dividend from a corporate division. Nevertheless, the regulations list pro rata distributions as evidence of a device.[12] Therefore, the "pro rata distribution" is an "unsafe harbor" for the taxpayer.

Subsequent Sale of the Stock.   As discussed earlier, an actual sale or exchange of the stock is evidence of a device. Moreover, the shorter the time interval between the receipt of the stock and the sale, and the greater the percentage of the stock sold, the stronger the evidence of a device.[13] However, the sale as evidence of a device can be overcome when subsequent, unexpected changes in circumstances (e.g., creditors demands, bankruptcy) necessitate the sale or exchange and thus counter a claim that the sale was part of a plan.[14]

A prearranged sale of the stock distributed in a spin-off is deemed strong evidence of a device[15] because the taxpayer has received assets from the corporation and still retains his or her relative ownership in the original corporation. After the distribution and sale, the seller has cash and

---

[11]Reg. §1.355-2(d)(2)(iii)(E). Reversing Rev. Rul. 70-225, 1970-1 C.B. 80.

[12]Reg. §1.355-2(d)(2)(ii).

[13]Reg. §1.355-2(d)(2)(iii)(A).

[14]See Ltr. Rul. 199914003 (December 15, 1998; Ltr. Rul. 9630033, several unforeseen changes in Controlled's business had adversely affected its ability to compete; sale pursuant to unsolicited offer.

[15]Reg. §1.355-2(d)(2)(iii)(B).

the same proportional interest in the distributing corporation, much the same as if the shareholder received a cash distribution.

Nature and Use of the Assets.   In *Gregory,* the parent corporation transferred investment assets to the subsidiary and distributed the subsidiary stock to Mrs. Gregory, who controlled the parent. Thus, Mrs. Gregory was able to sell the subsidiary stock and achieve a result that was much the same as receiving investment assets from the parent corporation and converting the investment assets to cash; moreover, the distributing corporation's business operations would be unaffected by the distribution. According to the current regulations, the existence of excess cash or highly liquid assets beyond the reasonable needs of the business of either the parent or the distributed corporation is suspect. Moreover, if the value of the transferred liquid assets relative to total assets is disproportionate to those of the distributing corporation, the device test will be brought into question.[16]

Also, as a general test, evidence of a device exists if the assets transferred could be sold without interfering with the operation of the business of the transferring corporation.[17] Thus, if the potential to sell the distributed stock is enhanced by the liquidity of the underlying assets, and/or the ability to sell the stock in one of the corporations (the spun-off corporation or the distributing corporation) without disturbing corporate operations, the device issue must be raised, whether or not the stock is sold.[18]

However, the regulations provide another safe harbor for the split-off. If the corporation that is being split off has excess cash because of the need to equalize values, the excess cash will not be evidence of a device.[19]

Example: D and C are equal shareholders in DC Inc. The corporation has net assets of $100 used to conduct two businesses:

---

[16]Reg. §1.355-2(d)(2)(iv)(A).

[17]Reg. §1.355-2(d)(2)(iv)(C). See Preamble to T.D. 8238, 1989-1 C.B. 92; *Wilson v. Commissioner,* 353 F.2d 184 (9th Cir. 1964).

[18]See section 355(g) for special rules that apply to the spin-off of an investment company.

[19]Reg. §1.355-2(d)(2)(iv)(B).

Business #1 requires net assets of $60, and Business #2 requires net assets of $40. For good business reasons, D and C decide to go their separate ways. The plan is that Business #2 will be transferred to a separate corporation, E Inc., and to equalize values, DC Inc. will transfer an additional $10 to E Inc. D will surrender his DC stock in exchange for the E stock. The fact that E Inc. has excess working capital will not be a device factor because it was necessary to equalize values in a split-off.

Finally, it should be noted that section 355(g) contains special rules that limit the availability of section 355 to investment companies, as opposed to corporations with an active trade or business.

Non-Device Factors

Strong Business Purpose.   The process of deciding the device issue is not simply a matter of counting the number of device factors and non-device factors that are present in the particular situation. The regulations imply that even though all of the device factors are present, the presence of a strong business purpose will decide the case in favor of the taxpayer. The regulations express this in a reverse manner: "The stronger the evidence of a device, the stronger the business purpose required" to satisfy the "not a device" requirement.[20] Obviously, the business purpose argument is strengthened by demonstrating the importance of the plan to the success of the business. The business purpose argument is further strengthened if "the transaction is prompted by a person not having a proprietary interest in the either corporation [e.g., regulators, creditors], or by other outside factors beyond the control of the distributing corporation."[21]

Publicly Traded.   The regulations include in the list of non-device factors the fact that the distributing corporation is publicly traded, and no shareholder holds a >5 percent interest in the stock.[22] However, in recent

---

[20]Reg. §1.355-2(d)(3)(ii)(A).

[21]Reg. §§1.355-2(d)(3)(ii)(A),(B).

[22]Reg. §1.355-2(d)(3)(iii).

years, there have been instances where a subsidiary borrowed from a third party and used the funds to pay a dividend to its publicly held parent and then the parent distributed the stock in the debt-laden subsidiary. Currently, the regulations protect the publicly held parent.

Domestic Corporate Shareholders. For a domestic corporate shareholder, whether the transactions qualify as a nontaxable spin-off, rather than being treated as a dividend from a domestic corporation, is of reduced significance, as compared to the individual shareholders. This is true because dividends received by a domestic corporation are eligible for the dividends received deduction (50 percent, 65 percent, or 100 percent, depending upon the percentage of stock ownership).[23] Therefore, Reg. §1.355-2(d)(3)(iv) provides that when the distributions are to other corporations, this is evidence that the transactions are not a device. However, it would seem that this exception would not apply when the corporate ownership is minor.[24] This appears true because the answer to whether the question of whether the spin-off is taxable applies to all shareholders and not on a shareholder by shareholder basis. On the other hand, a split-off requiring the distribution of control to a single corporation should not be consider a "device."

Examples of the Balancing of Factors

Strong Business Purpose but Sale of Stock

As discussed earlier, the strength of the business purpose and other factors must be balanced. Thus, a strong business purpose is strong evidence that the transactions were not a device. On the other hand, a sale of the stock soon after the spin-off is evidence of a device

The regulations provide several examples of the balancing of factors to decide the device issue. The first example is a spin-off so that a key employee can become a shareholder.[25] The business purpose is to enhance

---

[23]Reg. §243.
[24]Reg. §1.355-2(d)(5)(iv).
[25]Reg. §1.355-2(d)(4), Example 1.

the corporation's ability to retain the employee. The employer is a parent corporation and the key employee demands that he own stock in the parent; however, the parent owns stock in a valuable subsidiary, which makes the price of the parent's stock prohibitively expensive for the employee. To accommodate the key employee, the parent corporation spun off some of the business assets to a subsidiary and the employee purchased stock in the parent corporation from its controlling shareholder (Figure 4.1).

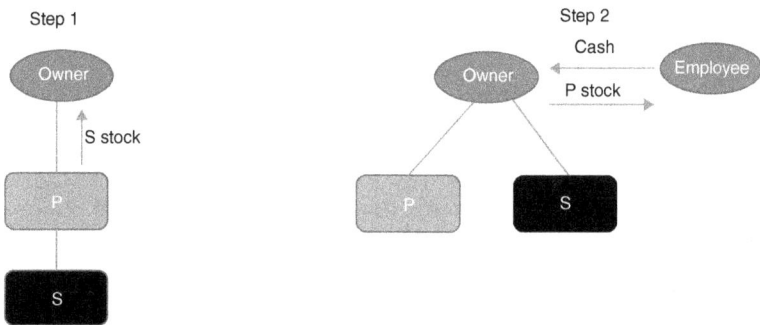

Figure 4.1 Spin-off and taxable sale of stock

As discussed in Chapter 3 at section "To Facilitate Employee Stock Ownership," a spin-off to facilitate key employee ownership of the stock is a strong business purpose. On the other hand, the fact that the controlling shareholder sold some of his stock was evidence of a device. The other consideration that went against the controlling shareholder's quest for capital gain was the fact that, as an alternative, the key employee could have purchased the stock from the parent corporation, rather than from the controlling shareholder.

The Service concludes in the example that the sale of the stock in the parent by its controlling shareholder was evidence of a "device" because the parent's shareholder sold his stock in the parent and received capital gains treatment.[26] As a result, the controlling shareholder recognized dividend income from the distribution of the subsidiary stock, as well as gain

---

[26]Note this same example is included in Rev. Rul. 96-30, discussing business purpose, discussed in the previous chapter. Compare this example to Reg. §1.355-2(b)(5), Example 8.

on the sale of the parent stock, and the parent corporation recognized any realized gain from the distribution of the subsidiary stock.

Strong Business Purpose, Pro rata Distribution, Liquid Assets

In an example from the regulations, the parent corporation operated two corporations, each with a different franchise business.[27] The franchisors required the parent to separate the businesses by distributing the stock of one of the corporations to the parent's sole shareholder. Therefore, a strong business purpose (a requirement of another party) for the distribution was present, which is an indication of no device. However, the distribution was pro rata, an indication of a device, and the corporations had some highly liquid assets. As in the *Gregory* case, the liquid assets were evidence of a device; however, the liquid assets were distributed proportionately between the two corporations, unlike in *Gregory*. The Service concluded that the strong business purpose overcame the pro rata distribution and the nature of the assets factors; therefore, the transactions were not a "device for distributing earnings and profits."

Another example in the regulations also involved a strong business purpose, a pro rata distribution of the stock and liquid assets.[28] The parent corporation's business was subject to State regulation, but the subsidiary was not. The State required the parent to dispose of the subsidiary, which was accomplished by distributing the subsidiary stock to the parent's shareholders on a pro rata basis. However, prior to the distribution, the parent transferred liquid assets to the subsidiary that were greater than the needs of the subsidiary's business operations, which was evidence of a device. Moreover, the transfer of the liquid assets was not made to equalize values, as is often done in a split-off.[29] The transfer of the nonbusiness assets as consideration and the pro rata distribution was seemed sufficiently strong evidence of a "device" to overcome the strong business purpose. Given the strong business purpose for distributing the stock, it seems apparent the transactions would not have been taxable,

[27]Reg. §1.355-2(d)(4), Example 2.
[28]Reg. §1.355-2(d)(4), Example 3.
[29]Reg. §1.355-2(d)(2)(iv)(B), as discussed in the previous chapter.

but for transferring the unneeded liquid assets. The result was the value of the stock received became taxable income and not merely the excess liquid assets.

As a follow-up on the previous example, instead of transferring excessive highly liquid assets, the parent purchased from the subsidiary assets unrelated to the subsidiary's business and the Service reached the same result as had the parent transferred excess cash. The transactions were considered a device for distributing earnings and profits.[30] It should be noted that in each of these two examples, none of the stock of the subsidiary (or the parent) was sold and thus at the time the decision was made as to the device issue no shareholder had attempted to achieve capital gains treatment from the stock, but the fact that the shareholders were able to readily convert the stock to cash was further evidence of a device.

Split-Offs

Generally, a split-off is not subject to the device test where the exchange would otherwise be taxed as a capital gain under the stock redemption rules.[31] The regulations contain an example of a split-off that does not enjoy this safe harbor. In the example, the corporation had three shareholders, A, B, and C and three businesses.[32] The corporation created two subsidiaries, X and Y, transferred a business to each of the two subsidiaries, and distributed the X and Y stock to shareholders B and C in exchange for their stock in the parent. (B and C each received 50 percent of the X stock and the Y stock.)

The split-off exception to the device test was not satisfied because either (or both) of the two shareholders whose parent stock was redeemed could sell his or her stock in one of the corporations without decreasing his or her interest in the other distributed corporation, an indication that the transactions were a device. Therefore, the transactions should be evaluated applying the device rules (decided in favor of the government), as well as the other spin-off requirements.

---

[30]Reg. §1.355-2(d)(4), Example 4.
[31]Reg. §1.355-2(d)(5)(iv).
[32]Reg. §1.355-2(d)(5)(v), Example 2. See also PLR 01949012.

The Balancing Act

Revenue Ruling 64-102[33] illustrates the balancing of considerations in reaching a determination regarding the business purpose of the corporate division and the device considerations. The ruling involved shareholders with strong differences of opinions about the management of the business. To resolve the conflict, shareholders owning one-third of the stock agreed to exchange their stock in the parent corporation for stock in a subsidiary corporation. The total value of the parent was $72, including a subsidiary operating a business with a value of $11. To equalize values, $13 cash was contributed to the subsidiary, thus increasing its value to $24, one-third of the value of the parent. The shareholders owning one-third of the parent stock surrendered their stock in the parent in exchange for a subsidiary with total assets of $24, of which $13 was cash. The elimination of the disagreement among the shareholders was a strong business purpose. The fact that over 50 percent of the subsidiary assets was cash (13/24), the essence of "highly liquid" indicated the transactions were a "device," but this was countered by the fact that if the split-off failed, the one-third shareholders would receive capital gains treatment under the stock redemption rules,[34] and, thus, the split-off was not device to convert dividend income into capital gain. Assuming all of the other section 355 requirements were satisfied, the strong business purpose and the absence of the device meant that the split-off was nontaxable.

In 2006, Congress added section 355(g) to limit the investment assets of the distributing or controlled corporation. The limitation generally applies to split-offs where the value of investment assets (including cash) exceed two-thirds of the total value of the assets of either the distributing corporation or the controlled corporation, and any person holds a 50 percent or greater interest in the distributing or controlled corporations. If the limitation is exceeded, section 355 does not apply and, therefore, both the corporation and the shareholder are subject to tax on the distribution.

---

[33]1964-1 C.B. 136.

[34]As a complete termination of an interest under section 302(b)(3).

Conclusions

The earlier discussion focused on the corporate division being used as a "device" for converting ordinary dividend income recognized when the stock is received into capital gains to be recognized from a sale of the stock at a time the shareholder is free to choose. But it is obvious that the division creates this opportunity and that opportunity is enhanced by the existence of highly liquid assets in the corporation, whether or not the shareholder takes advantage of the opportunity by selling the stock. On the other hand, the opportunity for achieving capital gain is lessened if a sale of the stock could interfere with business operations.

But the justification for not taxing the distribution must be a compelling business purpose for the division. Moreover, the section 355 requirements other than business purpose and absence of a device (i.e., distribution of control, the 5-year active conduct of a trade or business, continuity of interest) are relatively objective. When the objective standards are satisfied, whether the division is taxable often comes down to a weighing of the business purpose and device considerations: The stronger the business purpose, the more likely the section 355 requirements will be satisfied. A failure to satisfy the objective standards is fatal; therefore, business purpose and device are mute. As will be seen in the following chapter, satisfying the trade or business requirement is much more objectively determinable than the weighing of business purpose and device considerations.

CHAPTER 5

The Trade or Business Requirements

Introduction

To qualify as a nontaxable spin-off, the distributing corporation and the distributed (controlled) corporation must be actively conducting a trade or business immediately after the distribution.[1] Furthermore, the trade or business of both corporations must have been actively conducted throughout the 5 years ending on the date of the distribution.[2] The exception to this trade or business requirement is made for a corporate holding company that has no assets other than controlled corporations that are actively conducting a trade or business.[3]

The requirements for the active conduct of a trade or business present another barrier to the repeat of Mrs. Gregory's attempt to spin off investment assets. The 5 years of operations requirement prevents the corporation from investing accumulated funds in a trade or business to distribute to its shareholders.[4] Thus, in an indirect manner, the statute attempts to preserve the spin-off or split-off for the restructuring of the corporate organization undertaken for strong corporate business purposes rather than for their investors' desire to avoid taxes through the use of accumulated cash, to acquiring an unincorporated business, to be distributed. But the 5-year rule necessitates a definition of the active conduct of a trade or business, and a precise determination of when the trade or business was begun.

---

[1]Section 355(a)(1)(C).
[2]Section 355(b)(2)(B).
[3]Section 355(b)(1)(B).
[4]*McLaughlin v. Commissioner*, 115 T.C. 255 (2000).

The issue of when a trade or business begins has often arisen in the context of start-up costs,[5] research and development,[6] as well as section 355. The long-standing rule has been that the trade or business has not begun until the taxpayer begins "holding one's self out to others as engaged in selling."[7] However, the Supreme Court decided in *Snow v. Commissioner*[8] that this is not the correct starting point for determining when the trade or business begins for in all cases. Recently, the Internal Revenue Service (IRS) has expressed doubt as to whether this is the proper standard for the section 355 issue for a business that is in the process of developing its product.[9] But surely, the trade or business begins no later than when the entity begins to make sales, and section 355(b)(2)(C) provides that the measurement period ends on the date of the distribution.

Active Conduct of a Trade or Business

The active trade or business requirement distinguishes the corporation's activities of conducting a real business, seeking revenue from customers for providing them goods and services, from those of a mere owner of property that is being held for investment, as was the case in *Gregory*. According to Reg. §1.355-3(a)(2)(i), a trade or business exists when

> a specific group of activities are being carried on by the corporation for the purpose of earning income or profit....

Furthermore,

> the activities included in such group include every operation that forms a part of, or a step in, the process of earning income or profit. Such group of activities ordinarily must include the collection of income and the payment of expenses.

---

[5]Section 195.

[6]Section 174.

[7]*Richmond Television Corp., v. U.S.*, 345 F.2d 901 (4th Cir. 1965); Rev. Rul. 57-464, 1957-2 C.B. 244; Rev. Rul. 57-492, 1957-2 C.B. 247.

[8]416 U.S. 500 (1974).

[9]Rev. Rul., 2019-9, 2019-14 I.R.B. 925.

To satisfy the "active conduct" requirement, the corporation, through its employees, agents, and independent contractors, must perform a substantial portion of these activities. If the income is from the ownership of property, the corporation must provide significant services with respect to the operations and management of the property.[10]

Numerous cases have arisen regarding whether rental real estate produces trade or business income.[11] In general, the corporation is actively conducting a trade or business if the corporation's employees (or agents) seek tenants, maintain the property, and pay the property taxes and insurance. On the other hand, the corporation is not actively conducting a trade or business if the corporation leases its property under a long-term net–net lease (the tenant maintains the property and pays the insurance and taxes).[12]

In one example in the regulations, a corporation that owned and manages real estate rental property also owned vacant land held for future development.[13] Land development could be a trade or business, separate from owning and managing rental real estate, but the ownership of land for future development is not a trade or business. At the time of the spin-off of the land development business, the parent corporation was actively conducting its rental business, but the subsidiary's land development had not begun prior to the spin-off, and thus, the spun-off subsidiary was not engaged in the active conduct of a trade or business.[14] Therefore, the distribution was taxable to the corporation and the shareholder.

The 5-Year Requirement

Two Distinct Businesses

Trade or Business Internally Developed

It seems apparent that if the corporation actively conducts two distinct businesses, each with a source of revenue from different products or

---

[10]Reg. §1.355-3(b)(2)(iv)(B).

[11]See, e.g., *Rafferty v. Commissioner*, 452 F.2d 767 (1st Cir. 1971), *aff'g* 55 T.C. 490 (1970).

[12]Reg. §1.355-3(b)(5), Example 13.

[13]Reg. §1.355-3(b)(5), Example 2.

[14]Reg. §1.355-3(b)(5), Example 2. See also Reg. §1.355-3(b)(5), Example 3.

activities that were created by the same corporation, and the assets of one business are transferred to a separate corporation in exchange for all of its stock in a nontaxable section 351 transfer, the transferred business should retain its years of active conduct. This is the framework set forth in section 355(b)(2).

Section 355(b)(**2**)**Definition....** a corporation shall be treated as engaged in the active conduct of a trade or business if and only if—

A) it is engaged in the active conduct of a trade or business,
B) such trade or business has been actively conducted throughout the 5-year period ending on the date of the distribution,
C) such trade or business was **not acquired** within the period described in subparagraph (B) in a **transaction** in which gain or loss was recognized in whole or in part...

Thus, if the corporation owns and operates oil wells and grazes cattle on the same land, the corporation is conducting two distinct businesses, each with its own business history. Therefore, if, for good business reasons, it is necessary to separately incorporate the oil production and cattle operations, either the oil or cattle business could be transferred by the original corporation to a new corporation in exchange for all of the stock in the new corporation, which is nontaxable under section 351. But to distribute the cattle or oil corporation stock in a nontaxable transaction, there must be a business purpose for the distribution, and both the oil and cattle businesses must have been actively conducted for 5 years at the time of the distribution.

Assume that in the above example, the oil corporation operated the cattle business for at least 5 years before transferring the cattle business assets to the new corporation, which is temporarily a subsidiary of the transferring corporation. The cattle corporation acquired the cattle business in a transaction in a section 351 transaction and, thus, no gain or loss was recognized and therefore 355(b)(2)(C) was satisfied. This means that the new corporation's starting point for its trade or business is based on the transferring oil corporation's operations of the cattle business. It follows that if the time interval between the oil corporation entering the cattle business and the oil corporation distributed the cattle business stock was at least 5 years, the cattle corporation began with its temporal requirement of section 355 satisfied.

Acquired in a Taxable Transaction

On the other hand, if the newly formed corporation purchased an unincorporated operating cattle farm (i.e., cash paid for land, cattle, and equipment) in a taxable transaction for the seller, the 5-year count begins on the date of the purchase: The purchasing corporation does not inherit the unrelated previous owner's business history.[15]

The Taxable Section 351 Transfer or Reorganization

It should be noted that the business history transfers to the distributed corporation only if the transfer is not taxable "in whole or in part." Thus, for example, if the assets transferred were subject to liabilities in excess of the basis in the assets transferred, gain would be recognized[16] and thus the 5-year clock would not begin until the transfer to the controlled corporation.[17]

Five-Year Test: Nontaxable Division of an Existing Business

When the parent corporation creates what is generally viewed as a single business, actively conducts the business it created, and then transfers some of its assets to a new corporation that continues a portion of the original business, the result is that one business operating under one corporate shell is split and becomes two businesses operating under two corporate

---

[15]See *W.E. Gabriel Fabrication Co.,* 42 T.C. 545 (1964); S. Rept. No. 1622, to accompany H.R. 8300 (Pub. L. No. 591), 83d Cong., 2d Sess. 50-51 (1954); *McLaughlin v. Commissioner,* 115 T.C. 255 (2000).

[16]Section 357(c). The same results if the liabilities were deemed boot under section 357(b).

[17]Section 351 may not be the only possible means of getting assets to a subsidiary in a nontaxable transaction. The parent could create the subsidiary and acquired assets for the subsidiary through a reverse triangular A or reorganization. See section 368(a)(2)(C).

shells. The section 355 regulations may treat the new corporation as a successor of the original corporation's business history in the vertical splitting or horizontally slicing of a business.

The Horizontal Slice

A horizontal slice is illustrated in an example of a meat processor that created a separate corporation to conduct the sales function.[18] The regulation concluded that the tenure of the trade or business activities was shared by the newly formed corporation.

In another example, the corporation created a research department to develop new products. The research department did not receive revenue from customers. The research operations were spun off, and the subsidiary began conducting research for the parent corporation and other customers. The separate corporation benefitted from the knowledge and other intangible assets created before the transfer. The Service counted the research department's years of service to the parent corporation in determining whether the 5-year requirement was satisfied.[19] The results were the same in another example where a steel mill spun-off its captive coal company (the steel mill was the coal company's only customer).[20]

The Vertical Split

The vertical split is illustrated in Reg. §1.355-3(c), Example 4, which is a classic split-off. The two shareholders had operated a construction company for >5 years when they decided to go their separate ways. Therefore, some of the corporation's equipment and contracts were transferred to a separate corporation, and the stock of one of the original corporation's shareholders was surrendered in exchange for the stock of the newly formed corporation. The business activity history of the original corporation accompanied the transfer of the assets.[21]

---

[18]Reg. §1.355-3(b)(5), Example 10.

[19]Reg. §1.355-3(c), Example 9.

[20]Reg. §1.355-3(c), Example 11.

[21]Reg. §1.355-3(b)(5), Example 4. See also *Coady v. Commissioner*, 325 F.2d 28 (6th Cir., 1961).

Expansion of an Existing Business

As discussed above, in measuring the 5 years of active conduct of a trade or business, when the business is acquired in a transaction in which gain or loss was recognized (e.g., a purchase and the seller recognizes gain or loss), rather than in a nontaxable transaction (e.g., section 351 transfer or reorganization), the 5-year period cannot begin before the new owner causes the corporation to make sales. Thus, if a corporation engaged in a particular business simply buys an unincorporated business engaged in a different business and then incorporates the purchased assets and distributes the stock, the acquired business will not immediately qualify for section 355 treatment, regardless of how long it was operated by the previous owner. Instead, the clock starts when the new corporation begins selling its goods or services. The purchasing corporation must patiently wait for 5 years. However, the law distinguishes an isolated purchase from a purchase to expand an existing business.[22]

> …In particular, if a corporation engaged in the active conduct of one trade or business during that five-year period purchased, created, or otherwise acquired another trade or business in the same line of business, then the acquisition of that other business is ordinarily treated as an expansion of the original business, all of which is treated as having been actively conducted during that five-year period, unless that purchase, creation, or other acquisition effects a change of such a character as to constitute the acquisition of a new or different business.

If the taxable acquisition of the business assets is deemed an expansion of the corporation's existing business, the business history of the purchasing corporation carries over to the subsidiary when the acquired business is incorporated, as illustrated in Reg. §1.355-3(c), Example 8:

> For the past six years, corporation X has owned and operated hardware stores in several states. Two years ago, X purchased all of the assets of a hardware store in State M, where X had not previously conducted business. X transfers the State M store and

---

[22]Reg. §1.355(b)((3)(ii).

related business assets to new subsidiary Y and distributes the stock of Y to X's shareholders. After the distribution, the State M store has its own manager and is operated independently of the other stores. X and Y both satisfy the requirements of section 355(b) [five-year trade or business requirement]…

Some distinctions in the example should be noted:

- X's business had been operating for >5 years.
- X purchased the assets of an existing business.
- The assets were used by X in its business operations for 2 years before the assets were transferred to the new Y Corporation in a nontaxable transaction (section 351 transfer of assets for control of the corporation).

Similarly, a corporation operated a retail store in a downtown location for >5 years before it purchased land to build and operate a branch in a suburban area. Before construction was completed, the land was transferred to a newly formed corporation and the stock was distributed to the retail corporation's shareholders. The suburban location would enjoy benefits from the reputation developed at the downtown location. The 5-year business history of the downtown operations accompanied the movement of assets to the suburbs.[23] It should be noted that if the suburban store were deemed to be a separate business, the 5-year clock would not begin until the store began sales.

Finally, in Revenue Ruling 2003-18,[24] an incorporated automobile dealer sold and serviced a particular brand of automobiles (brand X) for >5 years before it purchased another dealer's assets and franchise to sell brand Y. For 2 years, the dealer sold and serviced both brand X and Y, but in the third year, the brand X assets were transferred to a new corporation and the stock was distributed to the brand X shareholders. The IRS concluded that the addition of brand Y was the expansion of a continuing business and, therefore, the years of the business X operations were

---

[23]Reg. §1.355-3(b)(5), Example 7.
[24]2003-7 I.R.B. 467.

attributed to the brand Y operations. The conclusion was that X's business history (which is >5 years) is attributed to the Y business. The manner in which the former owner used the assets did not matter. X was treated as though it acquired assets for use in its historical business, rather than as acquiring a new business.

Spin-Off of Owner-Occupied Real Estate

Frequently, shareholders realize that it would be preferable to separate the real estate used in the business from the other business assets. Two examples in the regulations are of a bank and its owner-occupied building, but with a portion of the building rented to tenants. In the first example,[25] the bank operates its banking operations out of first floor and leases to tenants the other nine floors. The bank employees manage and maintain the property. After 7 years of use in the banking and leasing businesses, the building was transferred to a newly formed corporation and the stock was distributed to the banking corporation shareholders. After the transfer, the building corporation employees managed the building, negotiated leases, sought new tenants, and repaired and maintained the building. The 7 years' trade or business activities of the real estate business were attributed to the new corporation. Therefore, the spin-off satisfied the active conduct of a trade or business requirement.

In the second example,[26] the bank occupied one and one-half stories of its two-story building for its banking business, and the bank rented the remainder of the building to a retailer who used the space for storage. After 9 years of banking and rental use, the bank transferred the building to a corporation and distributed the stock to the bank shareholders. The bank leased the one and one-half floors from the building corporation. Under the lease, the bank (rather than the corporation that owned the building) was responsible for maintaining its portion of the building, paying property taxes and insurance. In this case, the building corporation owned the property and collected the rent but did not perform trade or business activities (e.g., maintenance, seeking tenants); therefore,

---

[25]Reg. §1.355-3(c), Example 12.
[26]Reg. §1.355-3(c), Example 13.

the building corporation was not conducting a trade or business after the transfer and, as a result, the distribution of the stock was taxable. Note that if the building corporation had performed significant trade or business activities, the bank's prior use of the building would be a trade or business activity and the 5-year active conduct of a trade or business would have been satisfied.[27]

Summary and Conclusions

The above discussion distinguished the active conduct of a trade or business from the mere holding an investment for section 355 purposes. The discussion was also directed toward the section 355 trade or business requirement where multiple business activities are conducted inside one corporation and, for a good business purpose, some of these activities are placed in another corporation in exchange for a controlling interest in the transferee corporation. The issues were whether the business history was transferred along with the assets for purposes of determining whether the 5-year active conduct of trade or business requirement was satisfied before the distribution of the stock. Generally, if the activities originated inside the business, in the course of developing the business and are then transferred to a subsidiary in a nontaxable section 351 transaction, the history is also transferred. On the other hand, if a trade or business is purchased, the 5- year clock begins on the date of the purchase, unless the purchase is deemed an expansion of an existing business.

---

[27]See, J.W. Lee, "Active Conduct" Distinguished from Conduct of a Rental Real Estate Business, 25 Tax Lawyer 317 (1971–1972).

CHAPTER 6

Continuity of Interest

Introduction

The continuity of interest requirement is used to distinguish a reorganization from a sale or disposition of stock[1] and, in the context of a spin-off or split-off, continuity of interest means that the shareholders in the distributing corporation must retain sufficient ownership of the controlled corporation. According to the regulations,

> Section 355 requires that one or more persons who, directly or indirectly, were owners of the enterprise prior to the distribution [i.e., in a spin-off] or exchange [i.e., in a split-off] own, in the aggregate, an amount of stock establishing a continuity of interest in each of the modified corporate forms in which the enterprise is conducted after the separation.[2]

The degree of continuity required is "ownership of stock possessing at least 50 percent of the total combined voting power of all classes of stock entitled to vote, or at least 50 percent of the total value of shares of all classes of stock."[3]

It should be noted that the continuity of interest is a statutory requirement in the case of a section 368(a)(1)(D) reorganization, but its application to a section 355 distribution of an existing subsidiary is a product of the regulations. Moreover, much of the law relative to continuity of interest is derived from court decisions involving acquisitive reorganizations (e.g., mergers), whereas spin-off and split-offs are divisive transactions.

---

[1]Reg. §1.368-1(e)(1).
[2]Reg. §1.355-2(c)(1).
[3]Section 368(a)(2)(H), referencing section 304(c).

Therefore, the rules for section 355 transactions are not necessarily the same as those applicable to acquisitive transactions. In fact, when the Internal Revenue Service (IRS) issued new continuity of interest regulations for acquisitive reorganizations, it specifically provided that the rules do not apply to divisive reorganizations.[4]

The Regulations

The regulations illustrate when the continuity of interest requirement is satisfied and when it is not. In general, after the distribution, the historic shareholders (as a group) in the distributing corporation must continue to own at least 50 percent of the stock in the distributing corporation and 50 percent of the stock in the distributed corporation stock. Applying the test to the historic shareholders as a group permits a split-off (i.e., where shareholder relinquish all of his or her stock in the distributing corporation) to satisfy the test as well as a spin-off, as will be seen in the examples below.

All of the examples in the regulations involve split-offs. In a split-off, the shareholder's interest in one corporation increases, but his or her interest in another corporation decreases. Thus, it is possible for what appears to be a lack of continuity satisfies the requirements of section 355. The fact that in a spin-off the stock is distributed in proportion to the shareholder's stock ownership in the distributing corporation means that the distribution will not change the shareholder's relative interest in the two corporations and, therefore, continuity is generally not an issue. The exception to this general rule could occur if the distribution is followed by a change in ownership by one or more historical shareholders (e.g., a prearranged sale of the distributed stock), as will be discussed below.

In the discussion below, the term *historic shareholder* is used to signify that the shareholder's stock ownership in the distributing corporation was established before the spin-off occurred, such that the acquisition of the

---

[4]Reg. §1.368-1(b).

stock in the distributing corporation was not part of a plan to receive the distributed stock.

Examples from the Regulations

In the first example,[5] the corporate parent (X) and its subsidiary (S) are of equal, value and the parent has two shareholders (A and B) who each own 50 percent of the parent stock. In a split-off, the parent distributes 100 percent of the stock in the subsidiary, S, to shareholder B in exchange for his or her 50 percent of the parent stock.

Example 1 Corporations				
Shareholders	X before %	X after %	S before %	S after %
A	50	100		
B	50	0		100
X			100	
	100	100	100	100

Applying the regulations, the two original shareholders in the parent (the historic shareholders) had complete control of both corporations prior to the redemption because in the aggregate, they directly owned 100 percent of the stock in the parent and indirectly owned 100 percent of the subsidiary corporation. After the spin-off, the historic shareholders in the aggregated directly controlled both the parent and the subsidiary. Therefore, the continuity of interest requirement was satisfied.

In a second example,[6] C desires to purchase an interest in the parent, X, but does not want to indirectly invest in X's subsidiary, S. Shareholder A is willing to sell one-half of his X stock to C, and B is willing to accept all of the S stock in exchange for his 50 percent of the X stock.

---

[5]Reg. §1.355-2(c)(2), Example 1.
[6]Reg. §1.355-2(c)(2), Example 2.

The integrated transactions occur, and the ownership in X and S before and after the sales and exchanges is presented in the following table.

Example 2 Corporations				
Shareholders	X before %	X after %	S before %	S after %
A	50	50		
B	50	0		100
C		50		
X			100	0
	100	100	100	100

Note that C is not a historic shareholder, but became a shareholder as part of a plan, which included the distribution to B. After the integrated steps are completed, the historic shareholders (A and B) own 50 percent of the parent and 100 percent of the subsidiary stock, and according to the regulation, continuity of interest is satisfied. From this example, we can infer that the continuity of interest requirement is satisfied if the historic shareholders, A and B, together own as little as 50 percent of the stock in both X and S. (Note that X was required to distribute at least 80 percent of the S stock to B for the distribution to be nontaxable under §355. The continuity of interest percentage (50%) and the distribution percentage requirements (80%) differ.

In a third example in the regulations,[7] A and B each owned 50 percent of the X stock when X's wholly owned subsidiary, S, was split off to B (B exchanged the X stock for S stock) and then C purchased all of A's stock in X. C is not a historic shareholder. After the completion of the plan, C owns 100 percent of the X stock and B owns 100 percent of the S stock. Because none of the X stock is owned by the historic shareholders, the continuity of interest test was not satisfied.

---

[7] Reg. §1.355-2(c)(2), Example 3.

Example 3 Corporations				
Shareholders	X before %	X after %	S before %	S after %
A	50	0		
B	50	0		100
C		100*		
X			100	0
	100	100	100	100

*B's 50 percent of the X stock was redeemed, and C owns all of the outstanding X stock after the redemption.

The fourth example[8] is a modification of Example 2, where C purchased 50 percent of A's X stock and B received 100 percent of the S stock. However, in Example 4, C purchased 80 percent of A's stock in X (which was 40 percent of the outstanding X stock) and B exchanged his X stock for 100 percent of the S stock.

Example 4 Corporations				
Shareholders	X before %	X after %	S before %	S after %
A	50	20*		
B	50	0		100
C		80*		
X			100	
	100	100	100	100

*$(1 - 0.80)(50)/50 = 20\%$, and $(0.80)(50)/50 = 80\%$.

Therefore, after the C purchase and the B exchange, the remaining historic shareholder, A, owned only 20 percent of the X stock. The continuity of interest test was deemed failed. Thus, 50 percent ownership by the historic shareholders satisfies continuity of interest, but 20 percent ownership fails the test.

---

[8]Reg. §1.355-2(c)(2), Example 4.

Measuring Continuity

The above examples provide some guidance regarding the degree of continuity required and how it is measured. However, consideration must also be given to transactions that occurred before or after the distribution that may be deemed to be part of an overall plan. Whether the stock purchase and split-off were independent, or integrated steps in a plan, depends upon all the facts and circumstances.[9]

Predistribution Continuity

As mentioned above, all of the examples in the regulations are of split-offs, and the only way that continuity of interest would not be satisfied is if a new shareholder is not a historic shareholder; that is, a new shareholder acquired the parent stock before the distribution but under conditions that would require that the acquisition of the stock and the distribution should be treated as integrated transactions, and thus the shareholder with the newly acquired stock is not deemed a historic shareholder. For example, if the shareholder acquired parent stock under the condition that the subsidiary's stock will be distributed immediately after the purchase of the stock in the distributing corporation, the two transactions (purchase and distribution) would be treated as one and thus the shareholder was purchasing—and the corporation was selling—the stock in the subsidiary, which is not a section 355 transaction.

As a continuation of the above example, assume A owned 60 percent of X and B owned 40 percent before C purchased A's 60 percent of X. C's purchase was made on the condition that the S stock would then be distributed in a spin-off immediately after the purchase. B would receive 40 percent of the S stock and C would each receive 60 percent of the S stock, but C would not be considered a historic shareholder; the only historic shareholder included in the continuity of interest count is B, who has 40 percent of the stock in X and S, and thus the continuity of interest test (50 percent) is failed and the distribution is taxable to X, B and C.[10]

---

[9]See McDonald's of *Illinois v. Commissioner*, 688 F.2d 520 (7th Cir. 1982).

[10]It should be noted that in a section 368(a)(1)(A) reorganization, the continuity of interest requirement is 40 percent, but 50 percent under section 368(a)(1)(D) and section 355.

Example 4 Modified corporations				
Shareholders	X before %	X after %	S before %	S after %
A	60	0		
B	40	40		40
C		60		60
X			100	0
	100	100	100	100

Postdistribution Continuity

The continuity of interest requirement necessitates continuing equity participation by the historic shareholders in both the distributing and the controlled (distributed) corporation. A subsequent disposition of the stock in the distributing or controlled corporation raises issues as to whether the continuity of interest requirement is satisfied. A binding pre-arranged sale of >50 percent of the stock to occur after a spin-off would violate the objective continuity of interest requirement, as well as raising the device issue. Chapters 7 and 8 will discuss other postdistribution transactions that may affect continuity of interest.

Summary

In situations where the spin-off or split-off is between or among historic shareholders, the determination of whether the continuity of interest requirement is satisfied is based on an objective 50 percent of ownership test, as illustrated above. When other transactions occur, which may result in the reduction of the interest of a shareholder before the distribution, this reduces the degree of continuity and may cause a failure of the continuity of interest requirement. The taxpayer's only hope is the other transaction that causes a change of ownership was independent of the decision to complete the spin-off or split-off, and thus the new shareholder is "historic."

Postdistribution events may also affect continuity, as well as the determination of whether the distribution was a device to distribute earnings and profits. Although section 368(a)(2)(H) exempts postcontinuity dispositions of the stock for purposes of sections 368(a)(1)(D) and 351—thus allowing a transfer of assets for stock under a plan to distribute the stock—that exemption does not extend to the basic requirements of section 355. Thus, a postdistribution sale of the stock that was a part of the distribution plan may cause a violation of the continuity of interest requirement as well being considered a device to distribute earnings and profits.

CHAPTER 7

The Acquisition of Control of a Corporation Conducting a Business

Introduction

Chapter 5 discussed the 5-year trade or business requirement, and Chapter 6 focused on the continuity of interest requirement. The 5-year requirement was discussed in the context of a corporation that creates a trade or business that is eventually transferred to a subsidiary, and the stock in the subsidiary is distributed to the parent corporation's shareholders. The following materials are directed at situations where a 5-year holding period requirement is imposed on the corporate shareholder receiving the controlling interest as a distribution. In a sense, this extension of the stock ownership period requirement to the shareholder is another continuity requirement.

Section 355(b)(2)(D) and Section 355(d) impose a 5-year holding period to the shareholders in certain well-defined circumstances. These sections have interesting histories, which are important to gaining a broad understanding of the application of section 355 to corporate acquisitions involving "unwanted assets."

Purchase, Spin, and Sell

Background

Before the code was amended in 1988, tax practitioners developed a technique for disposing of the "unwanted assets" in an acquired corporation without recognizing gain.[1] The technique included a section 355 distribution, in the following scenario:

1. A corporation purchased a controlling interest in the stock of a corporation (the "target")
2. The assets that the acquiring corporation did not want to retain would be transferred by the target corporation to a subsidiary in a nontaxable section 351 transaction.[2]
3. The acquiring corporation would cause the target corporation to distribute the subsidiary with the unwanted assets to the acquiring corporation as a section 355 distribution.
4. The acquiring corporation would allocate its purchase price of the target stock between the target corporation stock and subsidiary stock received in the distribution.
5. The acquiring corporation would sell the stock of the unwanted subsidiaries for little or no gain.

Example: P Corporation desires to purchase all of the T Corporation stock. However, T Corporation has a wholly owned subsidiary, S, that is not wanted by P Corporation. P,T and S have actively conducted a trade or business for >5 years and T had owned S five years. The value of T without S is $1,000, and the value of S is $800. S owns assets with a basis of $100. T's basis in assets other than the S stock is $100 and T's basis in S is $100.

	Basis in assets	Fair market value
T, without S	$100	$1,000
T basis in S	$100	$800
S assets	$100	$800

---

[1] This technique was based on Rev. Rul. 74-5, obsoleted by Rev. Rul. 89-37, 1989-1 C.B. 107.

[2] The unwanted assets may already be in a subsidiary and, thus, no transfer was required.

Under the formerly used technique, P purchased the T stock for $1,800. T then distributed the S stock to P in a nontaxable spin-off. P was required to allocate its original $1,800 basis in the T stock between the T and S stock. The allocation was based on their relative market value:[3]

$$\text{P's basis in T} = (\$1,000/\$1,800) \times \$1,800 = \$1,000$$

$$\text{P's basis in S} = (\$800/\$1,800) \times \$1,800 = \$800$$

After the spin-off, P had a fair market value basis in the S stock and, therefore, was able to dispose of the unwanted S stock without recognizing gain ($800 selling price $-$ $800 basis) (Figure 7.1).

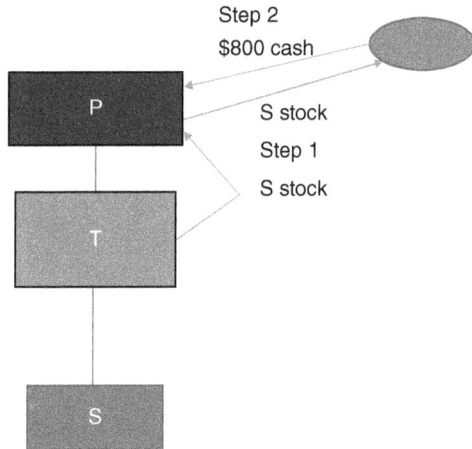

Figure 7.1 Purchase, spin, and sell

The simpler alternative to eliminating the unwanted assets would have been for T to sell the S stock; however, that would require T to recognize a $700 gain.[4]

---

[3]Section 358(b)(2).

[4]It should be noted that the sale of the S stock immediately after the distribution did not raise a "device" issue, Reg. §1.355-2(d)(3)(iv) exempts the domestic corporation from the device issue because if the distribution were not given section 355 treatment, the parent's receipt of the stock would be a dividend eligible for the 100 percent dividend received deduction, as discussed in Chapter 5.

The application of section 355 to the above transactions resulted in a deferral of income rather than an exemption from tax. This is true because the former T shareholders recognized the gain from the sale of their P stock (which included the $700 gain from S assets) and S recognized gain when it sells its assets with a basis of $100 and a value of $800. In fact, requiring T to recognize gain in this example would result in triple taxation of the $700 gain, because in addition to T's taxable gain, and the original T shareholders were taxed on their gain on the sale of the stock to P, T would eventually have taxable gain from the sale of the assets. However, the technique was being utilized after Congress enacted laws that generally required a corporation to recognize gain from distributing appreciated property to its shareholders and thus allowing the technique to continue "looked bad" to tax policy makers.

Purchase for Use in Redemption

Around the time that the purchase, spin, and sell technique became widely used, another technique for using section 355 to dispose of assets without recognizing gain came into view in *Esmark v. Commissioner*.[5]

Esmark was a publicly traded corporation undergoing a financial restructuring plan, which included stock redemptions. As part of the restructuring plan, Mobil Corporation agreed to purchase Esmark stock on the open market, and Esmark agreed to exchange all of its stock in a wholly owned subsidiary for Mobil's recently purchased Esmark stock. The value of the Esmark stock in the subsidiary was much greater than Esmark's basis in that stock. Under the Code as it existed when the transactions occurred, Esmark was not required to recognize gain from using appreciated property to redeem its stock.[6] The issue in the case was whether Esmark had constructively sold the subsidiary stock to Mobil; that is, the Internal Revenue Service (IRS) collapsed the steps, arguing that Mobil's purchase of the Esmark stock and the subsequent redemption was a constructive sale by Esmark of the stock in the subsidiary to Mobil for cash (Figure 7.2).

---

[5] 90 T.C. 171 (1988).
[6] Section 311(a), prior to the Tax Reform Act of 1986.

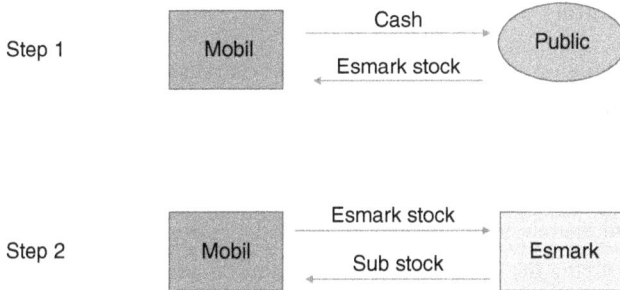

Figure 7.2 *Esmark-Mobil*

The IRS collapsed and rearranged the steps as though Esmark sold the sub-stock to Mobil for cash and Esmark used the cash to redeem its stock.

The Tax Court rejected the IRS argument and treated the Esmark-Mobil as a stock redemption. As mentioned above, under the law as it existed at that time, Esmark was not required to recognize gain from the distribution of the appreciated subsidiary stock in redemption of Esmark's stock. Because Mobil's basis in the Esmark stock was equal to the value of the subsidiary Mobil received, Mobil did not realize a gain from the redemption.

Section 355 was not raised in the Esmark case; however, it soon became apparent that the case had section 355 implications. That is, assuming the parent corporation distributed a controlling interest in a corporation that had actively conducted a trade or business for at least 5 years, and assuming all of the other section 355 requirements were satisfied, the transactions would be a tax-deferred split-off, rather than a taxable sale by Esmark and a stock redemption. Thus, a corporation could easily dispose of its unwanted but appreciated assets used in a trade or business for at least 5 years without recognizing gain, while reducing its outstanding stock by taking the following steps:

1. The parent locates a buyer for the parent's unwanted subsidiary owned for at least 5 years.
2. The buyer purchases a minority interest in the parent stock.
3. The parent exchanges the subsidiary stock for the buyer's parent stock in a section 355 split-off.

The Statutory Solution

The underlying policy concerns over the purchase, spin, and sell technique and the purchase for redemption technique was that appreciated assets were leaving the distributing corporation and neither the corporation nor the shareholder was recognizing gain. Moreover, it was not the historical shareholders in the corporation making the distribution that were receiving the distribution—which smacks of a discontinuity.

The key to the purchase and spin, as well as the purchase for redemption techniques was that the purchaser attained a stepped-up basis in the subsidiary stock without the former parent recognizing gain.[7] Congress's solution was to amend section 355(b)(2)(D) to require that when a corporation distributes a controlling interest in a corporation to another corporation, for the distribution to be nontaxable under section 355, the corporation receiving the stock (i.e., a split-off) must have owned a controlling interest in the stock in the distributing corporation at least 5 years the corporation that purchases a controlling interest in the stock in another corporation must have owned that stock for at least 5five years before it can be distributed nontaxable under section 355. This was an indirect solution to the basis issue (stepped-up basis and no gain), as well as a deterrent to other possible tax-avoidance techniques. The solution relied on an implicit assumption that after 5 years, the value of the purchased stock will have appreciated so that the basis allocated (determined by the stock purchase at least 5 years in the past) to the subsidiary will be less than the its value and, therefore, the acquiring corporation will have a realized gain on the sale. Thus, a corporate purchaser would be required to retain the unwanted assets for 5 years, just to attain a hoped for tax benefit that may not exist in the future.

Thus, after section 355(d)(2)(D) was added to the Code, as a requirement for a nontaxable section 355 distribution to another corporation:

1. The distributing corporation must have been actively conducting a trade or business for at least 5 years at time of the distribution.

---

[7]See, Preamble to Proposed Regulations, Guidance Regarding the Active Trade or Business Requirement Under Section 355(b) 72 FR 26012 (May 8, 2007).

2. The distributing corporation must have owned the stock in the controlled corporation for at least 5 years at the time of the distribution.
3. The controlled corporation must have been actively conducting a trade or business for at least 5 years at time of the distribution.
4. The corporate shareholder receiving the controlling interest as a distribution must have owned stock in the distributing corporation stock at least 5 years.

The failure to satisfy any one of these requirements means that the distribution did not qualify for section 355 and, therefore, the distributing corporation and the distributee corporate shareholder would be taxed on the distribution.

Purchase of Stock the Expansion of an Existing Trade or Business

In Chapter 5, the concept of the expansion of an existing business as opposed to the start of a new business was discussed. The distinction is important for a number of reasons, one of which is the requirement that the corporation whose stock is distributed must have actively conducted its trade or business for at least 5 years at the time of the distribution. But the distributing corporation must also have owned the stock at least five years, if the stock was acquired by purchase.[8]

> Example: P Corporation was in the hardware business in Iowa for 5 years when it purchased a hardware business in Kansas. If P purchased the assets, the Kansas store could be deemed an expansion of P's hardware business. The Kansas store could be incorporated and spun off immediately, and the 5-year active conduct of a trade or business requirement would be satisfied. On the other hand, if P purchased the stock of the Kansas hardware business the Kansas business stock could not be distributed in a nontaxable spin-off until P owned the stock at least 5 years.

---

[8]Section 355(a)(3)(B).

"Not Acquired by Purchase"

Section 355(b)(2)(D) does not apply if the stock in the distributing corporation is acquired in a totally nontaxable transaction (e.g., a corporate reorganization, a section 351 transaction, or liquidation of a subsidiary under section 332) and the target corporation owned the subsidiary at least 5 years prior to the acquisition and distribution. The reason for this exception is that the acquiring corporation will not attain a stepped-up basis in the stock of the target corporation or its subsidiary, as illustrated below:

> Example: P Corporation acquired T Corporation in a section 368(a)(1)(B) reorganization (a stock for stock exchange). The T shareholders exchanged their T stock with a basis of $400 for Pstock with a value of $1,200. T had a wholly owned subsidiary, S, with a basis to T of $100, and its fair market value was $300. T immediately distributed the S stock to P.

Because P acquired T in a nontaxable reorganization, P's holding period is not relevant. Under the general rules of sections 355(b)(1) and (2), P, S, and T must have been actively conducting a trade or business for at least 5 years at the time of the distribution. If these conditions are true, the distribution is nontaxable, regardless of how long P owned the T stock acquired in a nontaxable transaction.

In effect, when P acquired the T stock, P also acquired T's tax attributes, including T's 5-year period of actively conducting a trade or business. However, P also acquired T shareholder's basis in the stock received in the section 368(a)(1)(B) reorganization,[9] which was likely less than the value of the T stock, rather than the fair market value basis that would result in a purchase of the stock. Therefore, P would have taxable gain from the sale of the T stock, which means the nontaxable acquisition, spin, and sell technique was not effective in deferring tax.

Thus, section 355(b)(2)(D) eliminated the tax benefits of the purchase (taxable acquisition), spin, and sell technique. Acquisition by a

---

[9] Section 362(b).

nontaxable reorganization, spin and sell technique was still allowed because the spin-off will not result in a step-up in basis and, therefore, the sale by the distributee will result in taxable gain.

> Example: P Corporation acquired T Corporation in a section 368(a)(1)(B) reorganization (a stock for stock exchange). The T shareholders exchanged their T stock with a basis of $400 for P stock with a value of $1,200. T had a wholly owned subsidiary, S, with a basis to T of $100, and its fair market value was $300.

As a B reorganization, P's basis in the T stock is the same as the T shareholder's basis, $400.[10] Upon a section 355 distribution of S by T to P, the $400 basis in the T stock must be allocated by P between the T and S stock based on their relative fair market value. Thus, if T distributed the S stock to P in a section 355 distribution, P's basis in S would be $400 × ($300/$1,200) = $100; therefore, if P immediately sold the S stock, P would have a $200 taxable gain, the same as had T sold the S stock. No taxable gain was avoided in the section 355 distribution, even though no 5-year holding period was imposed on P.

Section 355(d): The One-Sided Taxable Distribution

Background

The *Esmark* case heightened IRS attention to the possible abuses of section 355. Section 355(b)(2)(D) addressed the *purchase, spin, and sell,* but that section's use was limited to situations involving corporate shareholders who receive in a distribution from another corporation at least 80 percent of the stock in the controlled corporation. Thus, for example, a corporation, individual, or partnership could purchase 60 percent of a corporation's stock and, a year later, use the target corporation's subsidiary that satisfied the 5-year requirement to redeem the other 40 percent of the target stock in a split-off (Figure 7.3).

---

[10]Section 361(b).

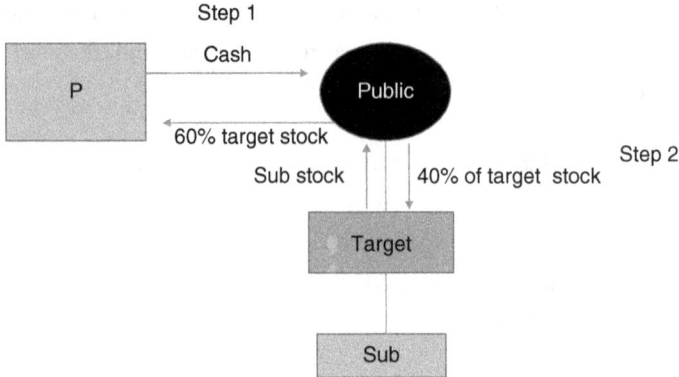

Figure 7.3 Target financing

Thus, P used the appreciated assets in C to finance the acquisition of D without C recognizing gain. After the redemption, P owns 100 percent of D.

Because of the imagined and unimagined possibilities for exploiting section 355, Congress decided that additional limitations on the spin-off and split-off were required.[11] Therefore, in 1990,[12] Congress added a new section 355(d) to require, in circumstances discussed below, that the shareholder (whether corporations, individuals, or other entities) must own the stock in the distributing corporation at least 5 years for the distribution to be nontaxable under section 355. Generally, the 5 years of ownership requirement applies if after a distribution, (1) a person holds a 50 percent or greater interest in the distributing corporation or the controlled corporation and (2) the 50 percent interest was purchased, or is attributable to stock purchased within 5 years of the distribution. If the ownership limit is met or exceeded, but all of the other section 355 requirements are satisfied, the distributee–shareholder is not taxed, but the distributing corporation is taxed on the distribution of the stock. The distributing corporation's taxable gain is the excess of the value of the stock at the time of the distribution and the distributing corporation's

---

[11]The step transaction doctrine could possibly be applied, that is, the IRS could argue that the stock purchase and redemption should be treated as integrated transactions. However, a more direct and consistent result could be achieved through a well-crafted statute.

[12]Pub. L. No. 100-647, §2004(k)(1).

basis in the property.[13]Thus, the effects of section 355(d) are deliberately asymmetrical: The distributing corporation is taxed (as though it sold the stock), but the distributee is not taxed on the distribution.

Recall that the section 355(b)(2)(D) 5-year ownership requirement applies to the corporate shareholder that receives a distribution of a controlling interest in another corporation. The 5-year ownership requirement prevents the corporation from purchasing the stock in another corporation, and selling off the target's unwanted or unneeded subsidiaries, without the acquiring corporation recognizing gain on the sales. Thus, the 5-year ownership requirement impedes a formerly used technique to shed unwanted assets or finance the acquisition in a tax-efficient manner. Section 355(d) hinders a parent corporation's ability to redeem its stock using the appreciated stock of its subsidiary without recognizing gain, as in *Esmark*. However, the section 355(d) formula differs from that of section 355(b)(2)(D).

The Section 355(d) Formula

The statute sets forth a complex formula that targets certain factual situations. A key variable in the section 355(d) formula is "disqualified stock" in the distributing corporation or the controlled corporation. If "disqualified stock" exists, the distributing corporation may be taxed on the distribution.

- Disqualified stock in the distributing corporation is any stock acquired by purchase within 5 years of the distribution.[14]
- Disqualified stock in the controlled corporation is stock acquired by purchase within 5 years of the distribution, as well as stock in the controlled received in a distribution, and is attributable to purchased stock in the distributing corporation purchased within 5 years of the purchase.[15]

---

[13]Section 355(d)(1). The stock distributed is treated a distribution of appreciated property under section 361(c)(2).

[14]Section 355(d)(3)(A).

[15]Section 355(d)(3)(B).

Another key variable is "disqualified distribution," which is any section 355 distribution if immediately after the distribution any person holds a 50 percent or greater interest in either the distributing or the controlled corporation.[16] The person owning the 50 percent or greater interest is a "disqualified person." The corporation must recognize any realized gain (the excess of the value of the distributed stock over the distributing corporation's basis in the stock distributed) from the distribution.[17]

Below is an example used in Chapter 5 dealing with the continuity of interest requirement, but the example could also have section 355(d) issues:

Example 1 Corporations				
Shareholders	X before %	X after %	S before %	S after %
A	50	100		
B	50	0		100
X			100	
	100	100	100	100

The distribution of the S stock to B, an individual, satisfied the continuity of interest requirement; therefore, B was not taxed on the distribution of S stock in redemption of his X stock. Assume, however, B purchased his 50 percent of the B stock within 5 years of the distribution. After the distribution, B owns at least 50 percent of the S stock; therefore, B is a "disqualified person." The distribution B received is "disqualified stock" because it is attributable to the X stock that B (a "disqualified person") acquired by purchase within 5 years of the distribution. Therefore, X Corporation must recognize gain (fair market value of the 100 percent of S stock less X's basis), but B is not required to recognize gain if all of the other section 355 requirements are satisfied. Also, if B were a corporation, because B owns >80 percent of the S stock after the distribution,

---

[16]Section 355(d)(4). A *50 percent or greater interest* is defined as "stock possessing at least 50 percent of the total combined voting power of all classes of stock entitled to vote or at least 50 percent of the total value of shares of all classes of stock."

[17]Section 355(d)(1).

section 355(b)(2)(D) would apply and the distribution would be taxable to both X and B Corporation. Note that if section 355(b)(2)(D) is violated, then section 355 is generally inapplicable—both the corporation and the shareholder must recognize gain.

It should be noted that in the case of a split-off, if only one shareholder's interest is being redeemed and that person is "a disqualified person," the corporation's entire gain is taxed. Moreover, if the distribution is a spin-off, the distributing corporation's entire gain is taxed, though some of the stock is distributed to shareholders who are not disqualified.

Below is an example of a spin-off and the two shareholders, A and B, respectively, owning 40 and 60 percent of the stock in the distributing corporation, X. Assume that A acquired her X stock by purchase within 5 years of the distribution, but B purchased his X stock >5 years before the distribution.

Example 2 Corporations				
Shareholders	X before %	X after %	S before %	S after %
A	40	40		40
B	60	60		60
X			100	
	100	100	100	100

The corporation is not subject to tax under section 355(d) because the shareholder owning at least 50 percent of the distributed stock, B, the X stock B received is not attributable to stock in the distributing corporation that was acquired by purchase within 5 years of the distribution.

On the other hand, if A had owned her X stock for at least >5 years and B owned his interest <5 years at the time of the distribution, the corporation would be required to recognize its entire gain on the all of the stock distributed—not just on the 60 percent of the stock distributed to B, the "disqualified person."[18]

---

[18]Sections 355(d)(1) and (2). House Report 101-964, p. 1086.

Attribution and Aggregation

Generally, when there is an ownership test, attribution and aggregation rules must be applied. Section 355(d) employs rules from sections 318, 267(b), and 707(b)(1).[19] Thus, in calculating the interest in the corporation, the taxpayer is deemed to own what he or she actually owns plus the stock owned by certain of his or her family members, stock owned by his or her controlled corporation, and stock owned by a partnership in which the taxpayer has an ownership interest. Moreover, a person who acquires by purchase at least 10 percent of the stock in a parent corporation is deemed to have acquired by purchase that same proportionate interest in its first and lower tier subsidiaries for the purposes of determining whether the person has an at least 50 percent interest in the corporation.

Purchase, Reorganization, Followed by Distribution

Consider the following example of a purchase of stock followed by a nontaxable reorganization and a distribution of a subsidiary's stock (Figure 7.4).

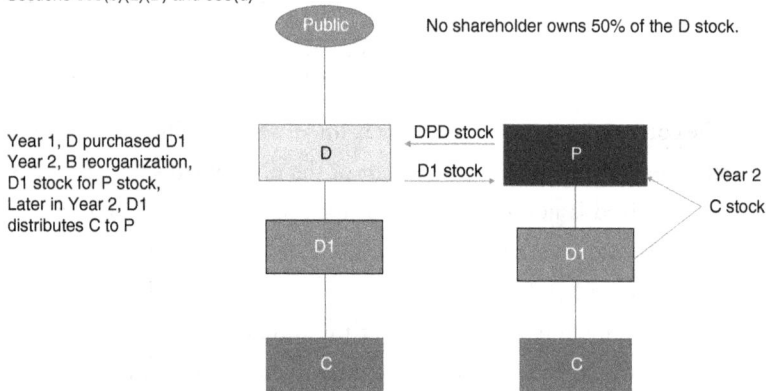

Figure 7.4 Purchase, reorganization, distribution

> Example: D1 owns all of the stock of C. D purchased all of the D1 stock for cash. Within 5 years of D's purchase of D1, P acquires all of the stock of D1 from D in a section 368(a)(1)(B) reorganization, and D1 distributes all of its C stock to P.

---

[19]Sections 355(d)(7) and (8).

As a result of the B reorganization, P's basis in D1 is the same as D's purchase basis.[20] Upon D1's distribution of the C stock to P, P must allocate its purchased basis in the D1 stock between the D1 and C shares. Therefore, P has a purchase basis in the C shares and P owns 100 percent of C after the distribution, and as a result, section 355(d) is violated[21]; however, because P attained a purchase basis in the controlling interest in the C stock that was purchased within 5 years of the distribution, section 355(b)(2)(D) applies and both P and D1 are taxed on the distribution.

The Application of Section 336(e) or 338(h)(10)

When the parent corporation distributes a controlling interest in the stock of its subsidiary as defined in section 1504(a)(2) in a taxable transaction to shareholders other than corporations, the parent corporation can elect under section 336(e) to treat the distribution as a sale of the assets of the subsidiary, the subsidiary will recognize gain (usually on a consolidated return), but the selling corporation does not recognize gain, and the subsidiary is allowed to step up its basis in its assets to fair market value. A similar election is provided under section 338(h)(10) if the controlling interest is distributed to a corporation. Therefore, when section 355(d) or 355(b)(2)(B) is violated, the section 336(e) or 338(h)(10) election can be made.[22] The effect of the election is to not tax the parent corporation on the distribution and instead tax the subsidiary on gain from the hypothetical sale of its assets, but the good news is that the subsidiary will enjoy a stepped-up basis in its assets.[23] The basis adjustments prevent triple taxation of the subsidiary's built-in gains; that is, in the absence of the election and basis adjustments, the built-in gains would be taxed as income to the selling corporate shareholder, the selling corporation shareholders (i.e., when their stock is sold), and the corporation whose stock is distributed.

Example: B, an individual, purchased 30 percent of the P Corporation stock in Year 1. P had a wholly owned subsidiary, T, that P

---

[20]Section 362(b).

[21]See, Reg. §1.355-6(b)3(vi), Example 4.

[22]The election can also be made if the distribution is subject to section 355(e), as discussed later.

[23]Reg. §1.336-2(b). See Preamble to T.D. 9619, I.R.B. 2013-24 (June 10, 2013).

purchased 5 years ago. In Year 2, P distributed all of the T stock in redemption of B's P stock. Section 355(d) applies because B purchased his P stock <5 years prior to the transfer, and after the distribution, B owned >50 percent of the stock in the T stock; therefore, P must recognize gain. In lieu of P recognizing the gain, under section 336(e), an election can be made to treat the transactions as though T sold its assets, T will recognize gain, but T's assets will be written up to their market value.

The election under section 336(e) or section 338(h)(10) is beneficial when the parent's basis in the stock is approximately the same as the subsidiary's net basis in its assets (subsidiary's basis in assets, less the subsidiary's liabilities). For example, if the parent has a much higher basis in the stock than the subsidiary's net basis in assets, the election may not be beneficial because the subsidiary's gain under the election would be greater than the parent's taxable gain without the election.[24]

When the Application of Section 355(d) Violates Its Intended Purpose

As discussed above, section 355(d) was added to the code to curb perceived abuses whereby a corporation distributes stock but was not required to recognize gain and a shareholder who recently purchased stock attained either

1. a stepped-up ("purchased") basis in the stock received as a distribution (e.g., as in the purchase, spin, and sale technique) or
2. an increased interest in the distributing or controlled corporation (i.e., percentage of outstanding stock) increased as a result of a distributed (e.g., *Esmark* and the split-off of another shareholder).

Congress recognized that the formula set forth in section 355(d) if literally applied could tax situations that were not intended. This was likely to happen because of the attribution and aggregation rules. Therefore, Congress authorized the Treasury to issue regulations to modify the

---

[24]The present value of the future tax benefits of the step-up in the basis of the subsidiary's basis in its assets must also be considered.

"purchase" rules to prevent taxing transactions in situations that would be inconsistent with the purpose of the statute. Treasury responded with the following regulation:

Reg. §1.355-6(b)(3)(i) *Certain distributions not disqualified distributions because the purposes of section 355(d) not violated—*

I. **(i)** *In general.* …. a distribution is not a disqualified distribution if the distribution does not violate the purposes of section 355(d). A distribution does not violate the purposes of section 355(d) if the effect of the distribution is neither—

    A. To increase ownership (combined direct and indirect) in the distributing corporation or any controlled corporation by a disqualified person; nor

    B. To provide a disqualified person with a purchased basis in the stock of any controlled corporation.

Thus, the regulations provide a two-prong test for determining when section 355(d) will not be applied: Section 355(d) will not be applied if a "disqualified person" neither (1) increases its direct or indirect interest in the distributing or controlled corporation nor (2) obtains a purchase basis in the controlled corporation stock. A disqualified person, as discussed above, is a 50 percent or greater shareholder in the distributing or controlled corporation after the section distribution.

Examples from the Regulations

The regulations provide 10 examples, some of which illustrate that under the facts a literal application of the statutes would not yield a result consistent with the purpose of the law, and therefore, the distributing corporation is not required to recognize gain. Below are some of the examples provided by the regulations.

Stock Distributed in a Spin-Off; No Purchase Basis

Example: D has a wholly owned subsidiary D1, and D1 has a wholly owned subsidiary, C. The D1 and C stock were acquired by purchase >5 years prior to the distribution. A purchased a 60 percent interest in D, and within 5 years of the purchase, D1 distributed all of the stock of its C stock to D.[25]

Under the attribution rules, A is deemed to have purchased 60 percent of the D1 and C stock when he purchased the D stock within 5 years of the distribution by D1. The distribution of C by D1 to D is attributable to stock purchased by A. Because A owns at least 50 percent of the stock in the distributee (D), the distribution is disqualified. However, A's interest in the distributing or controlled corporation did not change as a result of the distribution. Moreover, D's basis in the C stock is determined by D's basis in the D1 stock and is not determined by A's purchased basis in D stock. Because the purposes of section 355(d) are not violated, D1's distribution is not a taxable event (Figure 7.5).

Section 355(d)

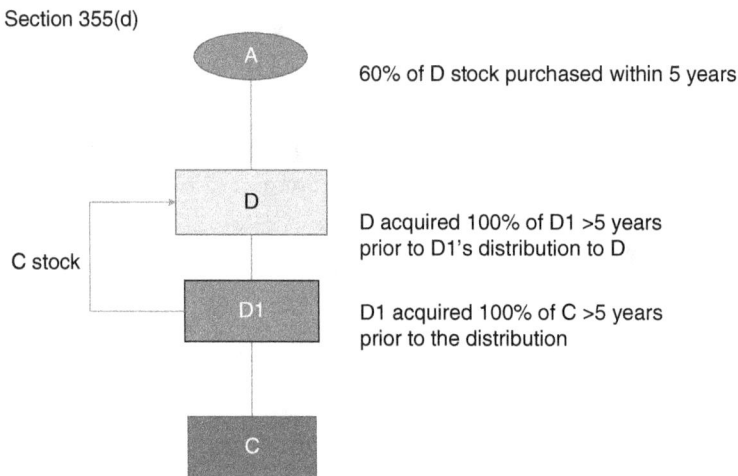

60% of D stock purchased within 5 years

D acquired 100% of D1 >5 years prior to D1's distribution to D

C stock

D1 acquired 100% of C >5 years prior to the distribution

Figure 7.5 No purchase basis

The second example is an extension of the previous example and demonstrates how section 355 addresses the lack of symmetry, that is, where one side of the transaction gets a stepped-up basis and the other side does not recognize gain.[26] In Figure 7.6, D, D1, and C are the members of an

---

[25]Reg. §1.355-6(b)(3)(vi), Example 1.
[26]Reg. §1.355-6(b)(3)(vi), Example 2.

affiliated group, and A purchased 60 percent of the D stock. Before A had owned his interest in the parent, D, for at least 5 years, D1 distributed C to D, and D distributed 60 percent of the C stock to A and the other 40 percent to other D shareholders (a pro rata distribution). The distribution of the C stock to D is not taxable, as discussed in the preceding example. Under the attribution rules of section 355, A, by his 60 percent ownership of D, was deemed to own 60 percent of D1 and C. Therefore, A's ownership in each of the corporations was not changed as a result of the distributions. However, the C stock is disqualified because A must allocate part of his purchase basis in the D stock to the C stock received, and assuming the C stock has appreciated, A's basis in the C stock will be "stepped up" (will be greater than D's basis in the C stock); therefore, D must recognize gain under section 355(d).

Section 355(d)

A's interest in D was purchased <5 years before the D1 distribution of C to D and before D distributed C.

60% of C   40% of C

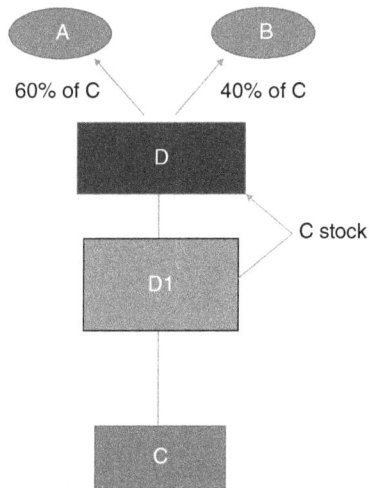

Figure 7.6 Stepped-up basis

Likewise, if the C stock were distributed to A in a split-off whereby A exchanged his D stock for C stock, taxing P on the distribution to A would not be inconsistent with the purpose of section 355(d) because A was a disqualified person (he owned at least 50 percent of D) who increased his ownership in the controlled corporation (100 percent of C was distributed to him) and he obtained a purchase basis in the distributed stock that was derived from his purchased basis in the D stock.[27]

---

[27]Reg. §1.355-6(b)(3)(i).

Purchase Basis and Stock Distributed in Spin-Off

The regulations contain another example[28] of a series of transactions that violated the section 355(d) requirements, and because of the stepped-up basis, rule was not "saved" as "not in violation of the purpose of section 355(d)" (Figure 7.7).

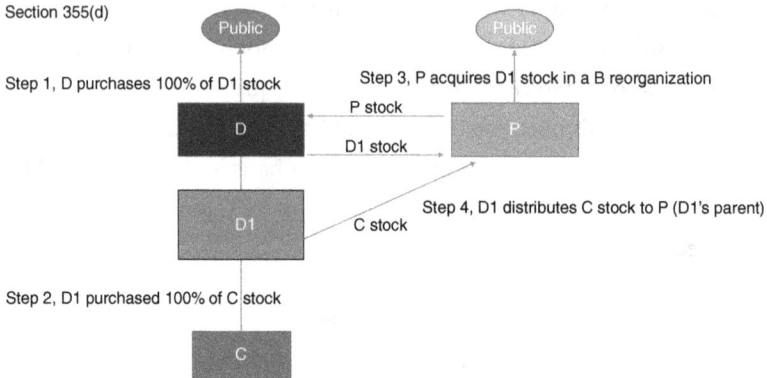

Figure 7.7 Stepped-up basis

Example: All within 5 years, (1) D purchased 100% of the D1 stock, (2) D1 purchased 100% of the C stock, (3) P acquired 100 percent of the D stock in a section 368(a)(1)(B) reorganization, and (4) D1 distributed the C stock to P.

As a section 368(a)(1)(B) reorganization, the D1 stock acquired by P is treated as acquired by purchase because P's basis in D1 is the same as D's, which is a purchase basis. D1's basis in C is also by purchase, as stated in the facts. Therefore, both D1 stock and C stock are disqualified, and P is a disqualified person because it owns at least 50 percent of the distributed stock. It follows that the distribution of the C stock does not satisfy section 355(d). In regard to whether applying the general purpose of section 355(d) test was satisfied, because of the attribution rules, P did not increase its ownership of C as a result of the distribution, but D1's basis in the C stock was a purchase basis; therefore, the distribution fails

---

[28]Reg. §1.355-6(b)(3)(vi), Example 4.

the "purpose tests" as well as the statutory test. It follows that D is taxed on the gain realized from the distribution.

Anti-avoidance Rule

Reg. §1.355-6(b)(4) is an anti-avoidance provision that generally allows the IRS to collapse the steps in a series of transaction to prevent tax avoidance. The regulations provide the following example (Figure 7.8).[29]

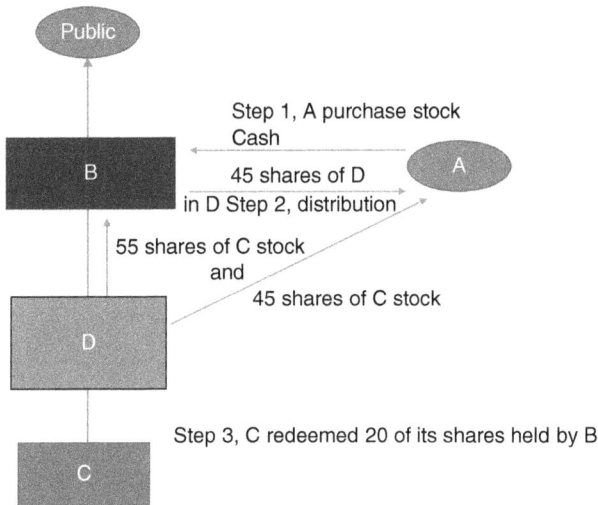

Figure 7.8 Antitax avoidance

Example: B purchased all the outstanding D stock and D purchased all of the outstanding C stock. The purchases occurred >5 years before step 1 in which A purchased 45 of the 100 outstanding B shares. Within 5 years of A's purchase of the D stock, D made a pro rata distribution of all of its C stock. Immediately after the distribution of the C stock, C redeemed 20 of its shares held by B.

Restating the facts for purpose of the section 355(d) analysis, A purchased 45 percent of the B stock and received a distribution of 45 percent of the C stock, within 5 years of the purchase. At this point, section 355(d) does not apply because no shareholder who purchased the stock

---

[29]Reg. §1.355-6(c)(4)(ii), Example (modified).

within 5 years of the distribution owns at least 50 percent of the distributing corporation, D, or the controlled corporation, C. (B acquired the D stock at least 5 years before the distribution.) However, when C redeemed 20 of its shares held by B, A's interest in the controlled corporation increased to $45/(100 - 20) = 56$ percent, and therefore, section 355(d) applied to the distribution.[30]

Summary

The determination of whether a distribution of a controlling interest in a corporation by its parent corporation will qualify as nontaxable under section 355 in part depends upon whether a continuity of interest exists after the transaction. That is, do the shareholders in the distributing corporation have at least a 50 percent interest in the distributor and the stock distributed? But there is more to it. Although this general continuity test may be satisfied, the transactions must also be tested under section 355(b)(2)(D) and section 355(d). Section 355(b)(2)(D) requires that in the case of corporate distributee, a corporation that receives a controlling interest (80 percent) in the distributed stock must have owned its stock in the distributing corporation for at least 5 years at the time of the distribution, and the distributing corporation must have owned the stock that is distributed for at least 5 years. If the corporate distribute owned the distributing corporation stock less than 5 years before receiving the controlling interest as a distribution, the distributing corporation and the distributee corporation must recognized any realized gain.

The transactions must also be tested for a section 355(d) violation. Under section 355(d), the distributing corporation may be taxed, if after the distribution a shareholder owns at least 50 percent of the stock in the distributing corporation or the controlled corporation. If the section 355(d) test is failed, the distributing corporation must recognize gain, but the shareholder does not recognize gain. Finally, if the section 355(d)

---

[30]In the present author's opinion, the same answer to this situation could be reached under Reg. §1.355-6(b)(3), applied in the previous example, and it is questionable whether the example in Figure 7.8 adds anything to an understanding of section 355(d).

general tests are not satisfied, the transactions may still be nontaxable if they do not violate the purpose of the statute. That is, if upon taking into account the attribution rules, the distribution does not result in an increase in the shareholder's ownership of the distributed stock, or the shareholder does not have a basis in the stock that is determined by the distributor's purchase price (rather than a carryover basis) in which section 355 is deemed satisfied. Thus, the journey through section 355 goal is arduous, but the consequences may be substantial.

CHAPTER 8

Corporate Division and a Related Reorganization

Overview

Events that occur before or after a spin-off or a split-off can threaten their tax consequences. The step transaction doctrine, in its various forms, evaluates the tax consequences of a series of related transactions by an overall assessment rather than evaluating each transaction as though it occurred independently.[1] Thus, as discussed in Chapter 4, if the shareholder sells his or her stock immediately after the spin-off, the sale is viewed as evidence that the distribution of the stock was a device to distribute earnings and profits to the shareholder. Also, a prearranged sale may result in a finding that the continuity of interest requirement is not satisfied. A post spin-off gift of the stock may indicate that the purpose of the spin-off was to serve the family financial planning of the owner rather than for a corporate business purpose.

This chapter is concerned with the frequently encountered situation in which a spin-off or split-off precedes or follows a nontaxable reorganization.[2] Such a pairing of transactions frequently occurs because the corporation being acquired in a corporate reorganization has assets that for business reasons are best excluded from the reorganization ("unwanted assets"), as illustrated in the *Morris Trust* case.[3]

---

[1] *McDonald's Restaurants of Illinois, Inc,, v. Commissioner of Internal Revenue*, 688 F.2d 520 (7th Cir. 1982).

[2] It should be recalled that generally, a spin-off or split-off pursuant to a reorganization is a safe harbor protecting the corporation and the shareholder from the device issue.

[3] 367 F.2d 794 (4th Cir. 1966).

The Morris Trust Case

In *Morris Trust*,[4] a state-chartered bank desired to merge into a National Bank. The State Bank owned an insurance business. Federal regulations prohibited a National Bank from owning an insurance business. Therefore, to make the State Bank suitable for the merger with the National Bank, it was necessary for the State Bank to dispose of the insurance business. This was accomplished as a spin-off: The insurance business was incorporated, and its stock was distributed pro rata to the State Bank shareholders. Then, the State Bank underwent a statutory merger with the National Bank as the surviving entity.

The Tax Court[5] and appellate court[6] in *Morris Trust* ruled the spin-off in conjunction with an acquisitive reorganization did not jeopardize the tax treatment of each other. The technical requirements for divisive and acquisitive reorganizations were much different from present laws. In the absence of any statutes directly on point, the fourth circuit's opinion was based heavily on tax policy, and the court could find no statutory barrier to combining a spin-off with an acquisitive reorganization that were both undertaken for valid business reasons. After the *Morris Trust* case, the spin-off soon became a commonly employed technique for a corporation to rid itself of unwanted assets as preparation for a merger.[7]

Then in the 1980s, some highly publicized transactions embellished the Morris Trust technique. For example, the business to be spun off would borrow before the spin off and distribute the cash to its parent, but the spun-off corporation would retain the liability. Although the spin-off and merger satisfied the letter of the law, the results appeared abusive to lawmakers who responded by enacting section 355(e) in 1997.[8]

---

[4]*C.I.R. v. Morris Trust*, 367 F.2d 794 (4th Cir. 1966).
[5]42 T.C. 779.
[6]367 F.2d 794 (4th Cir. 1966). But see *Curtis v. United States*, 336 F.2d 714 (6th Cir., 1964), which reached the opposite conclusion and was rejected by the fourth circuit.
[7]Rev. Rul. 96-30, 1996-1 C.B. 36. Rev. Rul. 68-603, 1968-2 C.B. 148.
[8]P.L. 105-206,§601(c)(2)(A-B).

Section 355(e): The Legacy of *Morris Trust*

Overview

In *Morris Trust*, the shareholders in the State Bank received part of the incorporated assets, the insurance business, and then exchanged the remainder of the State Bank assets for stock in the National Bank. Thus, the State Bank shareholders retained 100 percent of the insurance business, but a lesser interest in a banking business that included the original State Bank and National Bank businesses. The transaction caught the attention of Congress. The congressional committees that studied the case expressed concern that the underlying concept of continuity of interest, which generally applies to corporate reorganizations, was in doubt when a corporation spins off some of its assets to its shareholders, who, through a related merger, retain a less than 50 percent interest in the remainder of the corporation business.

> The Committee believes that section 355 was intended to permit the tax-free division of existing business arrangements among existing ["historic"] shareholders. In cases in which it is intended that *new shareholders will acquire ownership* of a business in connection with a spin off, the transaction more closely *resembles a corporate level disposition* of the portion of the business that is acquired.[9]

Thus, Congress's concern related to continuity of interest. A spin-off, followed by a merger, may result in the shareholders in the corporation spinning assets not having control of the remainder of the corporation. Thus, section 355(e) was added to the Code to better assure that a sufficient continuity of interest by the distributing corporation's shareholders exists to justify not taxing the transactions.[10]

---

[9]H.R. Rep. No. 105-148, at 462, S. Rep. No. 105-33, at 130-40 (1997) (current writer's emphasis added).

[10]M.L. Schler, Simplifying and Rationalizing the Spinoff Rules, 56 S.M.U.L. Rev. 239, at 271. The actual Morris facts were such that the State Bank shareholders owned >50 percent of the National Bank after the merger.

Section 355(e) applies when there is a distribution of stock, "which is part of a plan pursuant to which one or more persons acquire directly or indirectly stock representing a 50-percent or greater interest[11] in the distributing corporation or any controlled corporation." The section could also apply if the subsidiary whose stock was distributed (the "controlled corporation") engaged in a merger following the distribution or some other transactions involving the corporation's stock whereby the distributed corporation shareholders owned less than 50 percent of the stock in the distributed stock or successor entity, as discussed in a later portion of this chapter.

Effects on the Shareholders

The consequence of applying section 355(e) is that the distributing corporation must recognize gain on distributing the stock.[12] The realized gain is the excess of the value of the distributed stock received over the distributing corporation's basis in the stock.[13] However, the shareholders receiving the distributed stock are not taxed if all of the other requirements of section 355 are satisfied. The example below is the same as *Morris Trust* (Figure 8.1), except that in the actual case the State Bank shareholders owned more than 50 percent of the National Bank stock after the spin-off and merger.

> Example: T Corporation transferred assets to Newco in exchange
> for 100 percent of the Newco stock. T Corporation's basis in the
> assets (less liabilities) transferred was $30, and the fair market
> value (FMV) of the Newco stock received was $100. The Newco

---

[11]A *50 percent or greater interest* is defined as "stock possessing at least 50 percent of the total combined voting power of all classes of stock entitled to vote or at least 50 percent of the total value of shares of all classes of stock." Section 355(e)(4) cross-referencing section 355(d)(4).

[12]This is accomplished by rendering the stock in the subsidiary as not "qualified property" under sections 355(c)(2) and 361(c)(2), which makes the subsidiary stock appreciated "boot" property given. It would seem that given the continuity of interest rationale for section 355(e), the taxable transaction would be the reorganization where the shareholders lost control.

[13]Section 361(c)(2).

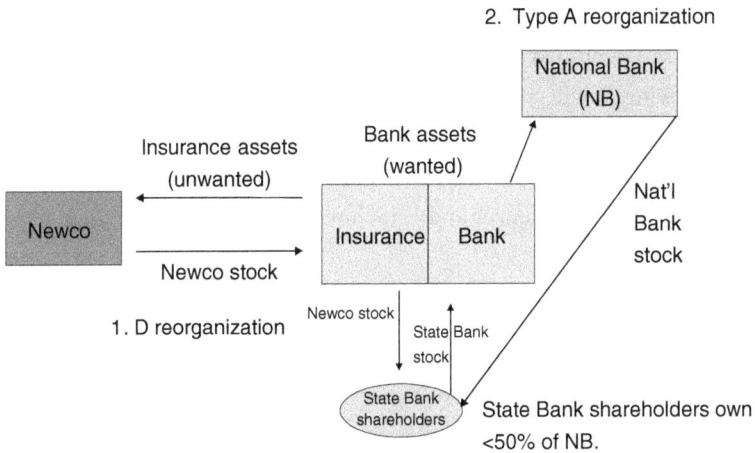

Figure 8.1 Morris Trust

stock was distributed to the T shareholders in a transaction that satisfied all of the section 355 requirements. Immediately after the distribution, the T shareholders exchange their T stock for stock in P Corporation, with the T shareholders owning 40 percent of the P stock after the exchange. Because the T shareholders owned less than 50 percent of the P stock after the reorganization, section 355(e) required T Corporation to recognize its realized gains, $100 − $30 = $70, from the distribution of the Newco stock. The T shareholders do not recognize gain and must allocate their basis in the T stock between the P and Newco stock. [14]

It should be noted that nothing in section 355(e) limits its application to a corporate division in combination with an acquisitive reorganization, as in *Morris Trust*. The division could be accompanied by a variety of possible transactions resulting in a loss of control of the distributing or controlled corporation, which could violate the general continuity of interest requirement, as illustrated below:

Example: A and B each have owned for more than 5 years 50 percent of the stock of T Corporation [and thus section 355(d)

---

[14]Section 355(d) would not apply because the stock is exchanged in a nontaxable transaction.

cannot be applicable]. D offered to purchase a controlling interest in T, if T will shed some unwanted assets. A and B agree to do the following: T will create C Corporation and spins off the unwanted assets, with A and B each receiving 50 percent of the C Corporation stock, in a transaction that meets the statutory requirements of section 355. Then, A and B each will sell 60 percent of their T stock to D.[15]

In these integrated transactions (the spin-off and the sale), each transaction was a part of the plan–a section 355 transaction occurred and the historic shareholders lost control of the distributing corporation. If section 355(e) applies, T Corporation must recognize gain from the distribution, A and B are taxed on their gain from the sales, but they are not taxed on the distribution. However, these transactions also violate the general continuity of interest requirement of the regulations, as discussed in Chapter 5, because A and B no longer control the distributing corporation, which means that section 355 does not apply. Therefore, A and B, as well as T Corporation may have taxable gain from the spin-off. In this case, the general rules would apply, rather than section 355(e). In *Morris Trust*, unlike the example above, the distribution and the reorganization each satisfied its own continuity of interest requirement.

Reverse Morris Trust

In the Morris Trust transactions, discussed above, the "unwanted assets" ("unwanted" by the merger partner) were placed in a corporation and spun off to the target corporation shareholders, and the remaining "wanted" assets were merged into the acquiring corporation in exchange for stock. In a reverse Morris Trust transaction, the wanted assets are placed in a controlled corporation (i.e., the wanted assets are transferred to a new corporation in exchange for all of the corporation's stock), whose stock is distributed to the parent corporation's shareholders and then the newly formed corporation is merged into the acquiring corporation. Section

---

[15]Note that if A and B owned their T stock <5 years at the time of the distribution, section 355(d) would also apply to the distribution, in which case section 355(d) controls. See section 355(e)(2)(D).

355(e) will apply and, thus, tax the distributing corporation (but not its shareholders) if all of the section 355 requirements are satisfied and the subsequent exchange of the spun-off corporation stock results in the shareholders in the distributing corporation owning less than 50 percent of the acquiring corporation's stock (Figure 8.2).

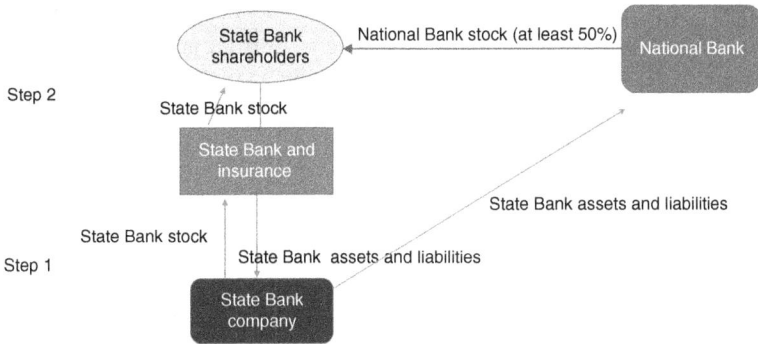

Figure 8.2 Reverse Morris Trust

Essentially, the tax laws relevant to the reverse *Morris Trust* are the same as the regular technique.[16] Thus, the distribution of a controlling interest in the spun-off corporation and a related subsequent change in ownership by the distributing corporation shareholders (as a result of an exchange of stock with the acquiring corporation) will be evaluated by the same standards as would be applied to a change in the ownership of the distributing corporation.[17]

> Example: P Corporation spun off S Corporation in transactions that satisfied the requirements of section 355. In a related transaction, S Corporation merged [in a section 368(a)(1)(A) reorganization] with Z Corporation, and the P Corporation shareholders received 25 percent of the Z stock. The subsequent merger does not affect the taxability of the spin-off, except in regard to the application of section 355(e). Thus, Z Corporation's basis in the stock received from S will be the same as S's basis. However,

---

[16]H. Rpt. 105-225, pp. 529-30; Rev. Rul. 98-27,1998-1 C.B. 1159.

[17]Joint Committee on Taxation, General Explanation of the Tax Legislation Enacted in 1998, p. 153, explaining section 368(a)(2)(H).

because the P shareholders own less than 50 percent of the stock in Z Corporation, P Corporation is taxed on the distribution as though it sold its assets to Z under section 355(e).

The merger was required to satisfy the section 368(a)(1)(A) requirements to exempt the corporation and shareholders from tax, and if so, the transactions must also satisfy the section 355(e) requirements to exempt the corporation from tax on the related spin-off from taxation. However, to exempt the distributing corporation from tax, the distributing corporation shareholders must own at least 50 percent of the stock in the acquiring corporation after the merger.

The Rebuttable Presumption

Section 355(e) requires measuring the shareholders ownership percentage. When a series of transactions are integrated into a "plan," the relevant percentage is calculated upon the completion of the plan. Whether the distribution and other events (e.g., a reorganization or sale of stock) are part of a plan that must be evaluated on the basis of all the transactions, rather on a transaction by transaction basis, generally depends upon the facts and circumstance.[18] Section 355(e)(2)(B) creates a rebuttable presumption that transactions occurring within 2 years before or after the distribution are parts of a plan and the results should be evaluated at the conclusion of the plan. Thus, to avoid section 355(e) the corporation making the distribution must bear the burden of proving that the various transactions are not part of an integrated plan.

For example, the distributing corporation may be planning a merger, which will require issuing new stock to the target shareholders. The acquiring corporation is also planning to redeem some of its outstanding stock. If the redemption occurs before the distribution, the value of the target relative to the distributing corporation will increase and, therefore, it would be more likely the target shareholders will own more at least 50 percent of the distributing corporation stock after the merger. Therefore, the distributing corporation would prefer to postpone the redemption

---

[18]See, e.g., Rev. Rul. 2005-65, 2005-41 I.R.B. 684.

until after the merger. On the other hand, the corporation may plan to issue new stock in addition to the stock issued in the merger. To protect the relevant ratio, the stock should be issued before the merger. In these two examples, when the corporation attempts to time its transactions to assure the 50 percent mark is not exceeded, the corporation must be prepared to rebut the presumption that the redemption was part of the plan and that the stock issuance was not a part of the plan.

Extensive regulations provide some guidance about whether a plan exists. That guidance focuses on preexisting understandings, agreements and negotiations, but provides safe harbors. The taxpayer can satisfy its burden of proof by demonstrating that during the 2-year period before the distribution, there was "no agreement, understanding, arrangement, or substantial negotiations" regarding the spin-off and acquisition.[19] In another safe harbor, the presumption is rebutted if there was "no agreement, understanding, arrangement, or substantial negotiations" within 1 year following the distribution.[20]

Transactions Involving the Distributing Corporation Stock

In General

It should be well understood that after a postdistribution merger, where the distribution and merger were integrated transactions, the distributing corporation shareholders must own at least 50 percent of the stock in the merged corporations to avoid the tax on the distributing corporation under section 355(e). However, what if the distribution corporation shareholders have a preexisting agreement to sell their stock in the merged corporations? The continuity of interest requirements for the acquisitive reorganization (under sections 368) would not be a problem according to the regulations, because those rules generally do not constrain postmerger actions by the shareholders.[21] But section 355(e) demands that pre- and post-reorganization events (2 years before and 2 years after the

---

[19]Reg. § 1.355-7(b)(2).

[20]Reg. § 1.355-7(d)(3). The regulations provide eight other examples.

[21]See Reg. §1.368-1(e)(8), Example 1.

distribution) must be taken into account in calculating the 50 percent requirement.

Commentators summarized the impact of the postdistribution transactions on the spin-off as follows: "The analysis as to the impact of post spin developments [involving the distributing corporation] is largely fact-intensive and tends to focus on two main inquiries: (i) How soon after the spin-off did such developments occur? and (ii) Were such developments planned or otherwise contemplated at the time of the spin-off?" [22]

> Example: A, B, C, and D are equal shareholders (25 shares each) in P Corporation. The original plan is for P to spin off S Corporation and then acquire T Corporation in a statutory merger, by issuing 75 new P shares for all of the T assets and liabilities. After distribution of S and the merger, the P shareholders would own 57 percent (100/175 shares) of the P Stock. At that point, all of the section 355 requirements were satisfied. However, B did not approve of the merger. To appease B, P Corporation agreed to redeem her stock as soon as the merger was completed, using T's excess cash. The redemption of B's stock decreased the historic shareholders (A, C, and D) ownership to 50 percent (75/150) and the T Corporation shareholders interest to 50 percent.

Because the merger and redemption were part of a plan that resulted in one or more shareholders acquiring a 50 percent or greater interest in P Corporation, P Corporation must recognize its gain from distributing the S Corporation stock. [23]

> Example: P Corporation's plan was to spin off S Corporation and then acquire T Corporation in a statutory merger. After the

---

[22]H.N. Beller and L.E. Harwell, "After the Spin: Preserving Tax-Free Treatment Under Section 355," https://us.evershedssutherland.com/mobile/portalresource/lookup/poid/Z1tOl9NPluKPtDNIqLMRV56Pab6TfzcRXncKbDtRr9tObDdEuS-pCs0!/fileUpload.name=/TAX355.PDF.

[23]See Joint Committee on Taxation, "General Explanation of Tax Legislation Enacted in 1997," JCS-23-97, at 201 (December 17, 1997).

merger, the P shareholders would own 60 percent of the P Stock. At that point, all of the section 355 requirements were satisfied. Soon after the merger, conditions changed and it became necessary for P to issue more stock to the public. After the issuing of additional P stock, the historic P shareholders owned 48 percent of the outstanding P stock.

The facts in the example, the changed circumstances, should enable P Corporation to overcome the presumption that the new stock issue was part of a plan that included the distribution, merger, and stock issue. Therefore, P Corporation shareholders owned more than 50 percent of the P stock after the merger and P is not taxed on the distribution.[24]

Exceptions to Section 355(e) [25]

Section 355(d) and (e) Overlap

As discussed in Chapter 7, section 355(d) applies when the stock acquired by purchase within 5 years of a distribution and combined with a distribution results in a shareholder owning at least 50 percent of the stock in the distributing corporation or the controlled corporation. If the spin-off or split-off violates section 355(d), the corporation is taxed, which is the same as the result if section 355(e) were applied as a result of a transaction subsequent to the distribution; that is, both sections tax the distributing corporation. Conversely, if section 355(d) is violated, the fact that the subsequent transactions did not violate section 355(e) will not salvage the distributing corporation from the tax on the gain. [26]

---

[24]See, J.L. Cummings, Jr. Counting Spinoff Stock Acquisitions, Tax Notes. August 26, 2019, p. 1363, for an exhaustive discussion of the counting rules applicable to section 355(e).

[25]See H.R. Rept. 100-220, Conference Report to accompany H.R. 2014 (1997), at pages 532–534; See Joint Committee on Taxation, "General Explanation of Tax Legislation Enacted in 1997," JCS-23-97, at 201 (December 17, 1997).

[26]Section 355(e)(2)(D).

Example: T, an individual, purchased 60 percent of P Corporation in Year 1. In Year 2, P distributed S to its shareholders. All P shareholders other than T owned their P stock at least 5 years at the time of the distribution. P's basis in T was $100, and its FMV was $500. P must recognize gain of $0.60($500 − $100) = 240, under sections 355(d) and 355(c)(2).

Immediately after the distribution, P Corporation merged with Mega Corporation and the P shareholders owned 40 percent of the Mega stock after the merger. Because the Mega Corporation shareholders acquired indirectly a 50 percent or greater interest in P Corporation, section 355(e) is also violated. Under section 355(e), P would recognize $500 − $100 = 400 gain [see sections 355(e) and 355(c)(2)].

Because both sections 355(d) and 355(e) otherwise apply, section 355(e)(2)(D) provides that only section 355(d) applies. Thus, P must recognize $240 gain.

Distributions within an Affiliated Group

Corporations that are members of a parent-subsidiary group (as defined in section 1504) are subject to special rules, including a 100 percent dividend received deduction and the ability to elect to file consolidated returns. Apparently, Congress concluded that it should avoid an overlap between section 355(e) and the special rules for parent-subsidiary groups that have a well-established history. Thus, 355(e) does not generally apply[27] to distributions within an affiliated group of corporations—that is, the distributing and controlled corporations are members of the same group after the completion of the plan (Figure 8.3).[28]

---

[27]As will be seen later, section 355(f) provides an exception to this general rule.

[28]Section 355(e)(2)(C). See H.R. Rept. 100-220, Conference Report to accompany H.R. 2014 (1997), at pages 532-534. The section 1504 group is expanded to include all 80 percent controlled corporations, including those ineligible for inclusion in a consolidated returns election by section 1504(b) (e.g., tax-exempt corporations).

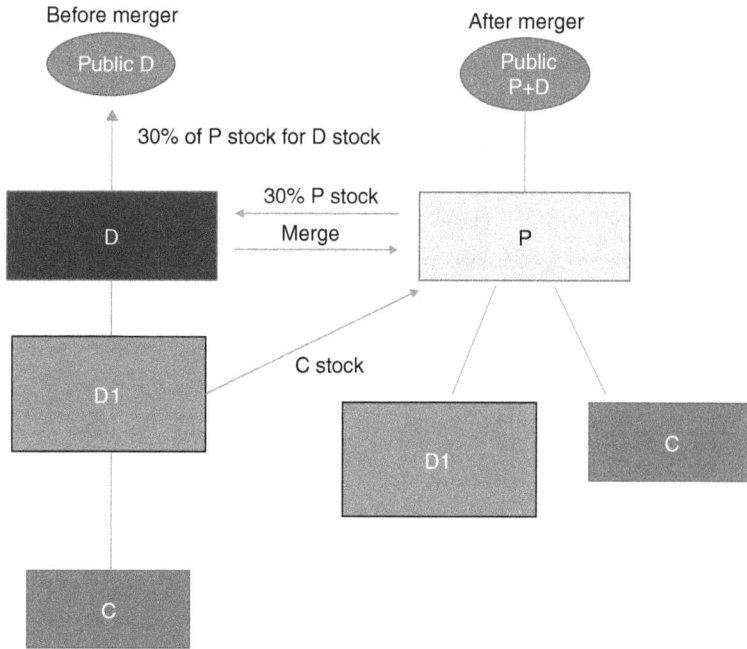

Figure 8.3 Distribution within the group

Example: D1 Corporation owned all of the stock of C when D Corporation purchases all of the stock of D1 for cash. After D had owned D1 for five 5 years [and thus sections 355(d) and 355(b)(2)(D) were not relevant], P acquires all of the D assets from D in a section 368(a)(1)(A) reorganization in which the D shareholders received 30 percent of the P stock. As part of a plan, D1 distributes all of its C stock to P.

Under the general rules of section 355(e), the D shareholders gave up indirect ownership of 100 percent of C for 30 percent of the P stock and, thus, D1 is taxable on its distribution. However, because the distribution is within the affiliated group of corporations, section 355(e)(2)(C) exempts the transactions.

Distribution Outside the Group as Part of the Plan

When a parent corporation has a subsidiary and the subsidiary also has a subsidiary, a second-tier subsidiary that the parent at the top of the organization desires to distribute to its shareholders, it is necessary for the first-tier subsidiary to distribute its subsidiary to the first-tier parent. Section 355(f) exempts from section 355(e) the internal spin-offs to the upper tier corporations that are part of a plan for a section 355(e) distribution outside the control group of corporations.

Example: P Corporation owns all the stock of subsidiary corporation S. S owned all the stock of subsidiary corporation T. S distributed all of the T stock to the P as part of a plan or series of related transactions in which P then distributed S to its shareholders and then P merged into an unrelated X Corporation. Corporations P, S, and T file consolidated returns.

	P	S	T
P basis in S		$100	
P basis in asset including S	$400		
S basis in T			$20
FMV	$500	$200	$75
FMV of S without T		$125	

After the merger, P shareholders own less than 50 percent of the voting power and value of the stock of the merged corporation (Figure 8.4).[29]

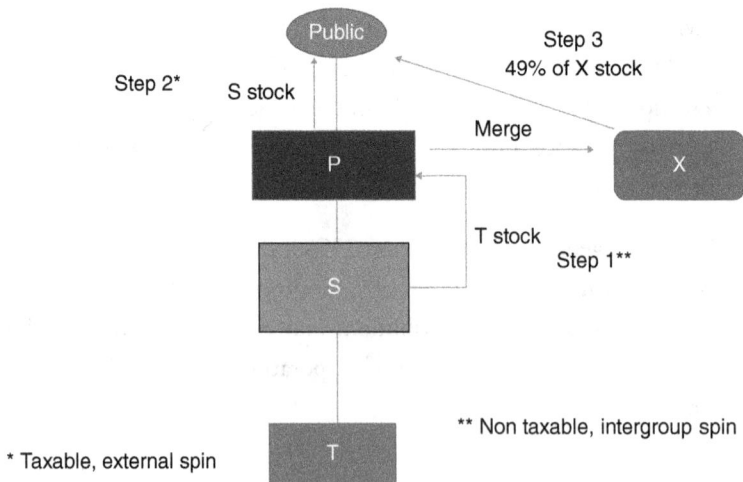

Figure 8.4 Distribution outside the group

---

[29]See H. Rept. 105-280 at p. 534.

Because S's distribution of T is part of a plan in which S is distributed by P outside the P affiliated group and P is then acquired under section 355(e), according to section 355(f), the intergroup spin-off by S of T to P is not subject to section 355(e). Thus, under the general rules of section 355, S's distribution of T to P is not taxable. P must allocate its basis between S and T based on relative FMV. The basis in S is calculated as follows:

$$\text{(Value of S without T)/(Value of S+T)} \times \text{Basis in S}$$
$$= (\$200 - \$75)/\$200 \times \$100 = \$62.50$$

Therefore, under section 355(e), P Corporation must recognize a gain of $125 − $62.50 = $62.50.

P's basis in T is $100 − $62.50 = $37.50. Therefore, P has a deferred gain in the T stock of $75 − $37.50 = $37.50.

On the basis of results under the consolidated return rules and without the application of section 355(f), S would recognize a ($75 − $20) = $55 distribution of T, and P would recognize a $45 gain from the distribution of the S stock; thus, the total $100 built-in gain in the S stock would be recognized. Section $355(f) defers $37.50 of the total gain that will be realized when the T stock is sold (i.e., when T leaves the X Corporation group).

Distributions with No Change in Ownership[30]

The Committee report provides an example involving a brother–sister corporation distribution followed by a merger:[31]

> Example: Individual A owns all the stock of P and X Corporations. P owns all the stock of a subsidiary corporation, S. Subsidiary S is distributed to individual A in a transaction that otherwise qualifies under section 355. As part of a plan, P then merges with X Corporation. Individual A aquired the X Corporation stock in a transaction unrelated to the distribution and merger (Figure 8.5).

---

[30]Section 355(e)(3)(A)(iv).
[31]See H.R. Rept. 105-280, Conference Report to accompany H.R. 2014 (1997), at pages 532-534.

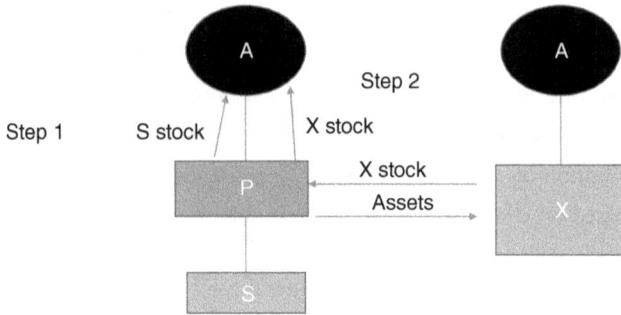

Figure 8.5 No change in ownership

The distribution and acquisition do not require gain recognition under section 355(e) because individual A owns directly or indirectly 100 percent of all the stock of both X, the successor to P, and S before and after the transaction. The same result would occur if P were contributed to a holding company, all the stock of which is owned by A.

Drop-Down and Split-Off

The Code exempts the distributing corporation from recognizing a gain when it creates a new corporation, which it then distributes to a historic shareholder in a split-off.[32]

> Example: Individuals A, B, C, and D have owned 25 percent of the stock of X for at least five years when X transferred part of its assets to Y Corporation in exchange for all of the Y stock, a non-taxable transaction under section 351. The Y stock was distributed to B in exchange for his X stock in a transaction that otherwise qualifies as a nontaxable split-off.

In this typical split-off, under the general provisions of section 355(e), the remaining X shareholders lost control of Y when it was distributed to B. Because the distribution was part of a plan by which B would attain 100 percent control of Y, under the general rules of section 355(e), X Corporation would be required to recognize gain. Section 355(e)(3)(A) (ii) exempts X from the application of the general rules.

---

[32]Section 355(e)(3)(A)(ii).

Predecessor and Successor Corporations

Morris Trust involved a spin-off of the insurance business and a merger of remaining state banking business into a national bank. The results were that the State Bank shareholders owned 100 percent of the insurance business and a lesser percent of the National Bank. Assume the order was reversed and that the State Bank merged into the National Bank and, as part of the plan, the National Bank spun off the insurance company after the merger. This would mean that the historic shareholders of the State Bank would not own 100 percent of the insurance stock. This is true because the National Bank would have shareholders other than the original State Bank shareholders. In both cases, the original State Bank corporation was divided and became a part of the National Bank. In the language of section 355(e)(4), the National Bank is the "successor" and the State Bank was the "predecessor," and according to the regulations, this means that the tax consequences of the division should be the same, regardless of the order of the transaction. Therefore, if the predecessor has a less than 50 percent interest in the successor after the nontaxable merger, that gain should be recognized, regardless of the ordering of events. Below is an example of a predecessor corporation from the regulations (Figure 8.6).[33]

> Example: Individual A owned 100 percent of State Bank stock, and individual B owned 100 percent of National Bank stock before State Bank merged into National Bank. After the merger, A owns 10 percent of the National Bank and B owned 90 percent of the National Bank stock. Following the merger, National Bank transferred the insurance business formerly owned by State Bank to a newly formed corporation C and distributes the C stock to A and B (10 percent and 90 percent, respectively). The distribution satisfied all of the section 355 requirements.

In this example, State Bank was much smaller than National Bank and, as a result, the State Bank shareholders had 10 percent of the ownership of the merged corporations. Nevertheless, the merger was nontaxable

---

[33]Reg. §1.355-8(h), Example 2, modified.

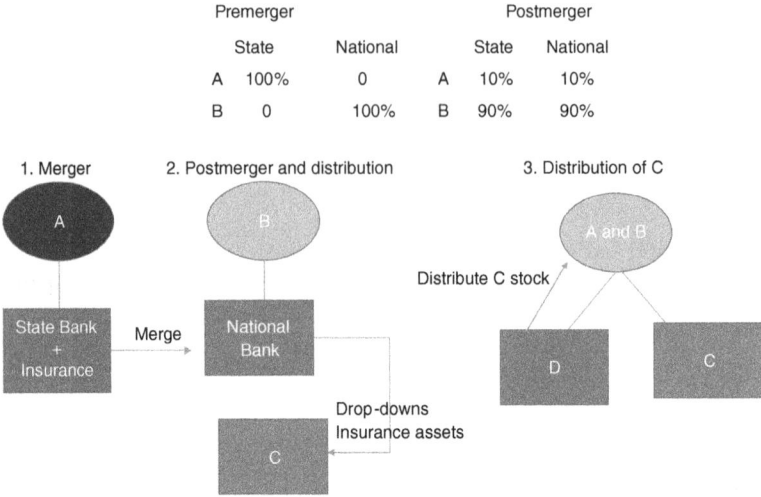

Figure 8.6 Predecessor and successor

under section 368(a)(1)(A). State Bank was the only source of the assets that were transferred from National Bank to the new C Corporation (as part of a section 368(a)(1)(D) reorganization), but as a result of the spin-off of the C stock, the original Sate Bank shareholders went from 100 to 10 percent ownership of the spun-off asset. Because the State Bank shareholder's interest in the insurance business decreased to less than 50 percent, section 355(e) applies and, therefore, the successor to State Bank, National Bank, must recognize gain equal to the difference between that C's basis in the insurance business (the same as State Bank's basis) and its FMV. Thus, the order in which the spin-off and reorganization (i.e., spin and merger, or merge and spin) occurred did not affect whether the transactions were taxable, although it did affect the economic result. (That is, if the insurance business were distributed before the merger, A would receive a greater percentage of the C stock.)

The Failed Section 355(e) Transaction

The corporation that is required to recognize gain under section 355(e) is deemed to have made a taxable distribution of the stock in the subsidiary. Therefore, as in the case of a tax incurred under section 355(e), the distributing corporation can elect under section 336(e) [in the case of individual distributees or 338(h)(10) for a controlling corporate distributee] to treat the disposition of the distributed stock as a sale of the corporation's assets.[34] Thus, the subsidiary becomes the taxpayer instead of the parent corporation (the distributing corporation). A benefit of the election is that the basis in the assets of the subsidiary can be written up to approximate their market value. The shareholders must receive at least 80 percent of the subsidiary stock for section 355 to apply.

> Example: P distributed the stock of a subsidiary with a basis of $100 and a FMV of $180. The subsidiary's basis in the assets was $170, the FMV of the assets was $250, and it had $70 in liabilities. In an integrated transaction, P merged with Z, and the P shareholders owned 25 percent of the Z stock. Thus, under section 355(e), P must recognize gain of $180 − $100 = $80. If a section 338(h)(10) election were made, the subsidiary would recognize gain of $250 − $100 − $70 = $80, and the subsidiary's basis in assets would be increased to $250, but P would not recognize from the distribution.

Summary and Conclusions

Section 355(e) is another of the obstacles to a corporation distributing property without the corporation or its shareholders recognizing income. When a section 355 distribution is made and, as a result of a related transaction, the shareholders ownership in the distributing corporation decreases to less than 50 percent, a tax must be paid based on the distribution, rather than the merger, the transaction that caused the loss of control. When the change in ownership and the distribution occur within 2 years of each other (before or after), they are presumed to be integrated as part of a plan, but that presumption is rebuttable. However, the analyses required to apply section 355(e) extends to transactions by the successor corporation that assumes tax attributes of the distributing corporation.

---

[34]Reg.§1.336-2(b)(2).

CHAPTER 9

Examples of Section 355 Transactions

Below are examples of corporate divisions and the analyses required to determine their tax consequences. The examples are intended to serve as a review of the earlier materials.

Spin-Off Followed by B Reorganization and Loss of Control

Corporation X had been engaged in the active conduct of two businesses (toy manufacturing and hand tool manufacturing) for over 5 years. Corporation Z, an unrelated corporation, desired to acquire the stock of X but was only interested in having X conduct the hand tool manufacturing business. This was accomplished pursuant to a plan under which X transferred its toy manufacturing business to a newly created corporation, Y, in exchange for all of the stock of Y, which was distributed pro rata to the X shareholders in a transaction that qualified as a reorganization within the meaning of section 368(a)(1)(D) and that met all of the requirements of section 355. Immediately after the distribution then acquired all of the outstanding stock of X in exchange solely for 23 percent of the voting common stock of Z. X remained in existence as a wholly owned subsidiary (Figure 9.1).

The exchange of the X stock for the Z stock is a reorganization within the meaning of section 368(a)(1)(B), which defines a *reorganization* as the acquisition by one corporation, in exchange solely for its voting stock, of stock of another corporation if, immediately after the acquisition, the acquiring corporation has control of such other corporation.

Revenue 70-434

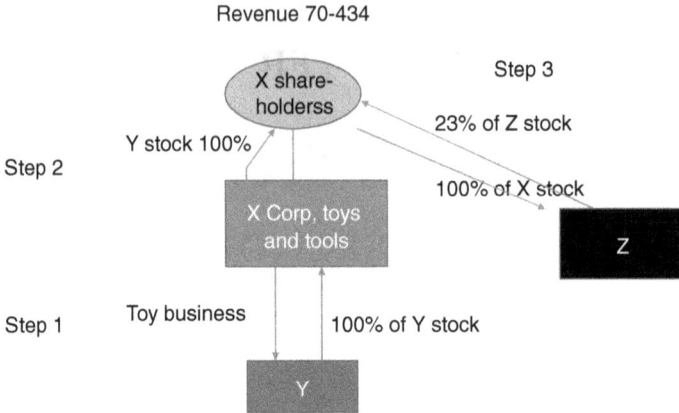

Figure 9.1 B reorganization with loss of control

However, because the X shareholders own less than 50 percent of the Z stock, the distribution of the Y stock is taxable to X under section 355(e), because both the distribution and the B reorganization were pursuant to a plan and were undertaken within 2 years. As a distribution taxable to X (but not to its shareholders), X can elect under section 336(e) to treat the transactions as a sale of the toy assets and Y will recognize gain, rather than X recognizing gain, the basis in the Z assets may be stepped up.[1]

Revenue Ruling 2017-9, Situation 1, North–South Transfer

P operates business A, and P's wholly owned subsidiary, D, is a mere holding company for its subsidiary C, which operates business B. For good businesses, P wanted to change the corporate structure so that Business A would be directly owned and operated by D, and P would directly own C. Businesses A and B had been actively conducted by P and C for over 5 years. Under the plan, P transferred Business A to D and D transferred all of the C stock to P (Figure 9.2).

The Internal Revenue Service (IRS) considered the plan as a two-step process: a section 351 transfer of Business A to D and a section 355

---

[1]Rev. Rul. 70-434, 1970-2 C.B. 83.

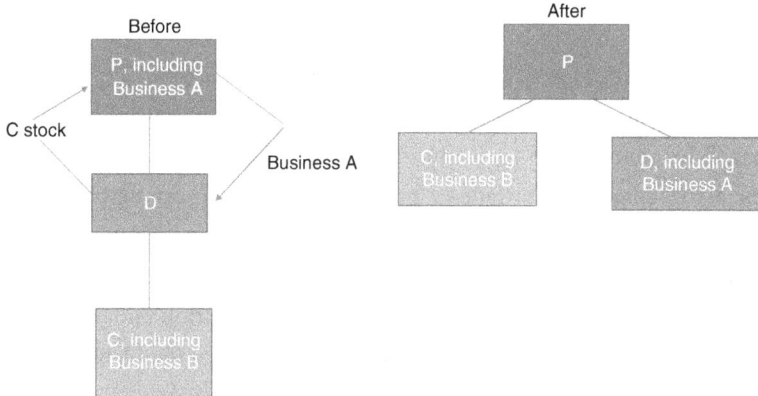

Figure 9.2 Revenue Ruling 2017-9, situation 1, north–south transfer

distribution of the C stock to P. If the steps were collapsed, the transactions become a taxable exchange by P of its Business A for D's stock in C.

The IRS concluded that the transfer of Business A to D was a valid section 351 transfer.[2] Moreover, D satisfied the section 355(b) trade or business requirement through its ownership of C (which conducted a trade or business). Because P, D, and C satisfied the active conduct of a trade or business requirement, the distribution of the C stock by D was a valid section 355 distribution.

The key to the success of the section 355 transfer was the IRS agreeing that the transfer to D qualified for section 351, separated from the distribution of the C stock. A section 351 transfer is often necessary to set the stage for a spin-off or split-off. In a typical section 368(a)(1)(D) plan, P transfers Business A to a newly formed subsidiary, D, and P distributes the D stock to the P shareholders and, thus, the transferor is no longer in control of the corporation. In the ruling, the IRS held that "the transfer (i.e., §351 transfer) is respected as a separate transaction, regardless of whether the purpose of the transfer is to qualify the distribution under section 355(b)." See section 368(a)(2)(H).

---

[2]Because P owned 100 percent of the D stock prior to the transfer, receiving more stock would not change P's ownership. Rev. Rul. 70-240, 1970-1 C.B. 81.

Revenue Ruling 2017-9, Situation 2

P owns all the stock of D, which owns all the stock of C. D has been engaged in Business A for more than 5 years. C has been engaged in Business B for more than 5 years. Business A and Business B each constitutes the active conduct of a trade or business within the meaning of section 355(b). On Date 1, C distributes cash and appreciated property to D. On Date 2, D transfers to C appreciated property, and D distributes all the C stock to P in a transaction qualifying as a reorganization under sections 368(a)(1)(D) and 355. C and D planned and executed the Date 1 transfer in pursuance of the plan of reorganization (Figure 9.3).

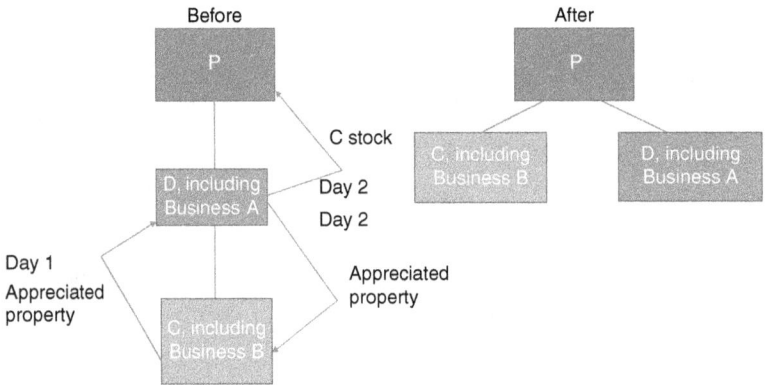

Figure 9.3 Revenue Ruling 2017-9, situation 2, north–south transfer

In this second situation in Revenue Ruling 2017-9, the service ruled that D's transfer of assets to C, followed by the distribution of the C stock to its shareholders, was a spin-off in the form of a nontaxable section 368(a)(1)(D) reorganization. Unlike most section 368(a)(1)(D) reorganizations, this involved a transfer of property to an operating subsidiary, rather than a newly formed corporation. However, the property received by D from C in a reorganization was boot received, and because it was not distributed to its shareholders, D must recognize gain under section 361(b)(1)(B). Although the ruling did not explain why the property that D received was treated as boot, rather than a dividend, according to Reg. §1.1502-13(f)(3)(i), because D no longer controlled C upon completion of the integrated transactions, D's interest in C was completely terminated by D's distribution of the C stock. Thus, the boot was more akin to sales proceeds than a dividend, which is consistent with the redemption rules.

Morris Trust, Section 355(e) with a Section 336(e) Election

Y Corporation has a subsidiary, Z, which is "unwanted" by the Y shareholders (all individuals) but "wanted" by X Corporation. In Step 1, Y distributed the Z stock to its shareholders in a transaction that qualifies for section 355. Within 2 years of the spin-off, X and Z underwent a statutory merger, and the Y shareholders exchanged their Z stock for 40 percent of the X stock, and thus, the Y shareholders did not control X (Figure 9.4).

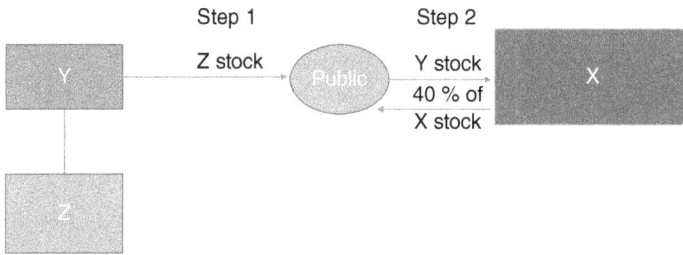

Figure 9.4 Reverse Morris Trust, section 355(e) with a section 336(e) election

Thus, section 355(e) renders Y taxable on the distribution but the distribution was not taxable to the Y shareholders. Because Y must otherwise recognize gain from the distribution, Y can elect under section 336(e) to treat the distribution of the Z stock as a sale of the Z assets and step-up Z's basis in those assets and Y will not be required to recognize its realized gain from the distribution of the Z stock. However, Z must recognize gain on the deemed sale of assets under section 336(e).

Reverse Morris Trust and C Reorganization

Revenue Ruling 2003-79 is referred to as the "born-to-die" ruling because the subsidiary was created to facilitate a section 368(a)(1)(C) merger of the subsidiary into an unrelated corporation (Figure 9.5).

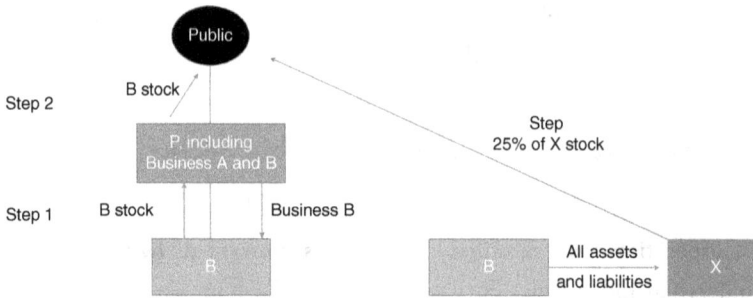

Figure 9.5 Revenue ruling 2003-79 reverse Morris Trust and C reorganization

P Corporation has conducted Business A and B for more than 5 years. X Corporation desired to acquire the Business B, but not Business A. As part of a plan, P created B Inc. and transferred all of the Business B assets and liabilities in exchange for all of the B stock. P distributed all of the B stock to the P shareholders. Immediately after the B stock was distributed, B transferred all of its asset and liabilities to X Corporation in exchange for 25 percent of the X stock, and liquidated. The B shareholders (who were also P shareholders) received the 25 percent of X stock. Because the historic P shareholders did not receive at least 50 percent of the X stock (the P shareholders lost control of B), P Corporation is taxed on the distribution of the B stock to the P shareholders under section 355(e). Because P is required to recognized gain, P is treated as acquiring the B stock by purchase under section 338(h)(3) and can elect to write up the basis in the B assets under section 336(e). The exchange of B assets for X stock satisfied the requirements for a section 368(a)(1)(C) reorganization because substantially all of the B assets were transferred to X. Therefore, the P shareholders were not taxed on the distribution of either the B shares or the X shares.

The major issue in the ruling was whether the step transaction doctrine would be applied to the spin-off because of the prearranged merger of B with X. If the steps were collapsed, the P shareholders never had control of B. The Service ruled that the steps would not be collapsed; that is, the Service reasoned that according to the legislative history of sections 355(e) and 368(a)(2)(H), the steps should not be collapsed and thus B Corporation transferred "substantially all" of its assets as required for a section 368(a)(1)(C) reorganization. Therefore, the spin-off and C reorganization were not taxable to the shareholders, but P was taxed on the spin-off [section 355(e) applied] because the P shareholders received less than 50 percent of the X stock. The Ruling should be compared to the Elkhorn Coal Company case, a *Morris Trust* (not reverse) transaction—section 355 spin-off with a C reorganization.

Elkhorn Coal Co., *Morris Trust*, and Failed C Reorganization

In *Helvering v. Elkhorn Coal Company*, 95 F.2d. 732 (4th Cir., 1937), the company spun off the unwanted assets and transferred the wanted assets for stock in an attempted C reorganization. Because of the spin-off of assets as part of the plan for the C reorganization, the court found that the section 368(a)(1)(C) reorganization requirements were not satisfied because P did not transfer "substantially all" of its assets to X. The court collapsed the spin-off with the C reorganization and concluded that because of the spin-off, by which P disposed of some of its assets, less than substantially all remained for the attempted C reorganization. As was seen in Revenue Ruling 2003-79, discussed above, by spinning-off the wanted assets and then completing a section 368(a)(1)(C) reorganization the "substantially all test" may be satisfied, but section 355(e) may apply and thus the distributing corporation must recognize gain (Figure 9.6).

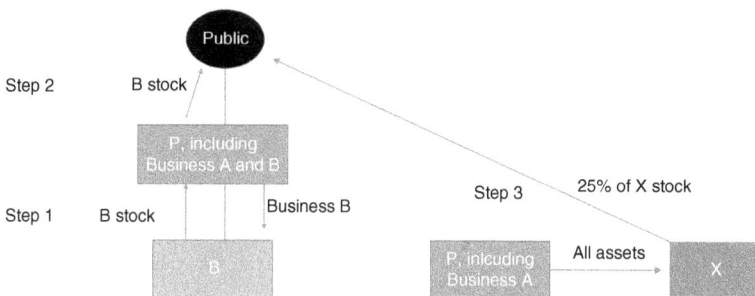

Figure 9.6 *Elkhorn Coal Co., Morris Trust, and failed C reorganization*

Split-Off by a Publicly Traded Corporation

Split-offs are common among closely held corporations, but much less so among publicly held companies. However, DuPont disposed of Conoco as a split-off. DuPont acquired Conoco, another publicly held corporation, in a nontaxable reorganization. More than 5 years later, DuPont engaged in some corporate restructuring and made an offering to all of its shareholders that they could exchange their DuPont stock for Conoco stock, but sufficient DuPont shareholders had to accept the offer so that at least 80 percent of the Conoco stock would be exchanged. The 80 percent requirement was satisfied, so DuPont was able to substantially reduce its outstanding stock without the use of any cash and without taxable gain (Figure 9.7).

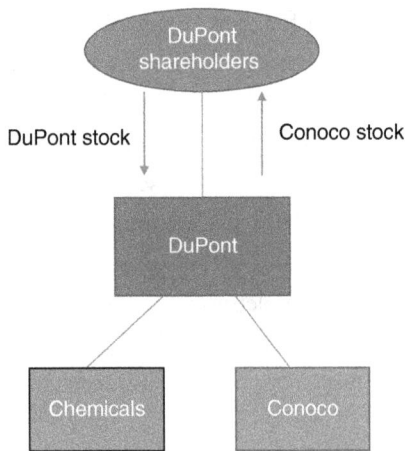

Figure 9.7 Split-off by a publicly traded corporation

Brother–Sister Split-Off

Individuals A and B each owned 50 percent of the X Corporation and Y Corporation stock. The corporations are of equal value. A and B decided to go their separate ways. One means of accomplishing the goal would be for A to exchange his or her X stock for the other parties Y stock. However, that would be taxable transaction. Under the plan, A and B each transferred his or her Y stock to X Corporation in exchange for additional

X stock—nontaxable under section 351. Then B transferred his X stock to X and received all of the Y stock in exchange. See Arthur W. Badanes, 39 T.C. 410 (1962) (Figure 9.8).

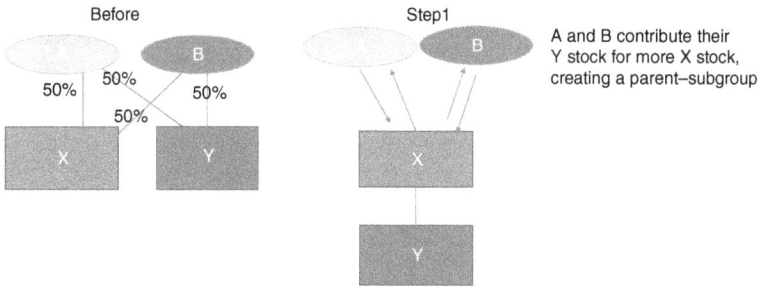

Figure 9.8 Brother–sister split-off

The key to the above plan satisfying section 355 is for the section 351 transactions to be recognized as valid.

Brother–Sister Split-Off

A and B were equal shareholders in X and Y Corporations when they decided to go their separate ways. The total value of the X stock was $3,700, and the value of the Y sock was $700. The total value of each shareholder's interest in the two corporations was $2,200. A and B encountered complexities in dividing the businesses because of the differences in size. Each business satisfied the active conduct of a trade or business requirement. The final plan was to create Z Corp., and X transferred to Z Corp. with a value of $1,850 and Y transferred assets with a value of $350. This was a section 351 transfer. X Corporation received 84 percent of the Z stock, and Y Corporation received 16 percent of the Z stock (Figure 9.9).

B received 84 percent of the Z stock in exchange for 84 percent of his X stock, and 16 percent of the Z stock in exchange for his Y stock. The receipt of the Z stock for X was a section 355 distribution of control by X and thus was nontaxable. The Z stock received for Y stock was taxable

Revenue Ruling 77-11

X and Y Corporations are equally owned by A and B.
The fair market values are X = $3,700 and Y = $700

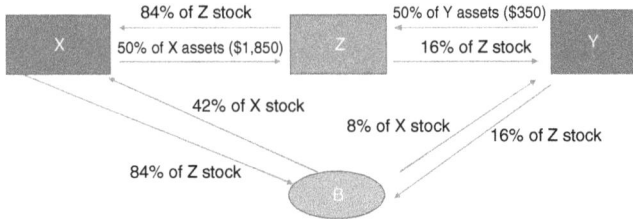

Figure 9.9 Brother–sister split-off, unequal values

to Y and B because Y did not distribute control of Y and thus was not a section 355 distribution. See Rev. Rul. 77-11, 1977-2. I.R.B. 13.

The more tax-efficient technique for the brother–sister split-off was illustrated in Figure 9.8. That is, A and B could contribute their Y stock to Z Corporation (a newly formed corporation) in exchange for Z stock. Other X assets could be contributed to Z Corporation to bring the value of Z and X is equal. Then, one of the shareholders could exchange his or her 50 percent of the X stock for 100 percent of the Z stock.

Expansion of an Existing Business

For more than 5 years, D had engaged in the active conduct of operating a retail shoe store, under the name D Inc. Throughout this period, D Inc. sales were made exclusively to customers who frequented its retail stores in shopping malls and other locations. D Inc.'s business enjoyed favorable name recognition, customer loyalty, and other elements of goodwill in the retail shoe market. D Inc. created an Internet website and began selling shoes at retail on the website. To a significant extent, the operation of the website drew upon D's existing experience and know-how. The website was named "D.com" to take advantage of the name recognition, customer loyalty, and other elements of goodwill associated with D and to enhance the website's chances for success in its initial stages. Eight months after beginning to sell shoes over the web, D transferred all of the website's assets and liabilities (all of which include the significant assets and goodwill associated with the website's business) to new subsidiary D Com. and distributed the D Com. stock to the D shareholders. The onsite and web products were the same. Although selling shoes over the web required some know-how not associated with operating a retail store, such as familiarity with different marketing approaches, distribution chains, and technical operations issues, the website's operation drew to a significant extent on D Inc.'s existing experience and know-how, and the website's success would depend in large measure on the goodwill associated with the D Inc. name. Therefore, the creation by D Inc. of the Internet website did not constitute the acquisition of a new or different business. Accordingly, it was an expansion of D's retail shoe store business, all of which was treated as having been actively conducted throughout the predistribution period. Therefore, D Inc. and D Com. both satisfied the 5-year active conduct of a trade or business requirement of section 355(b). Assuming all of the other section 355 requirements were satisfied, D could distribute D Com. without D or the D shareholders recognizing gain, even though the website sales began fewer than 5 years ago. See Prop. Reg. 1.355-3(d)(2), Example 19 (Figure 9.10).

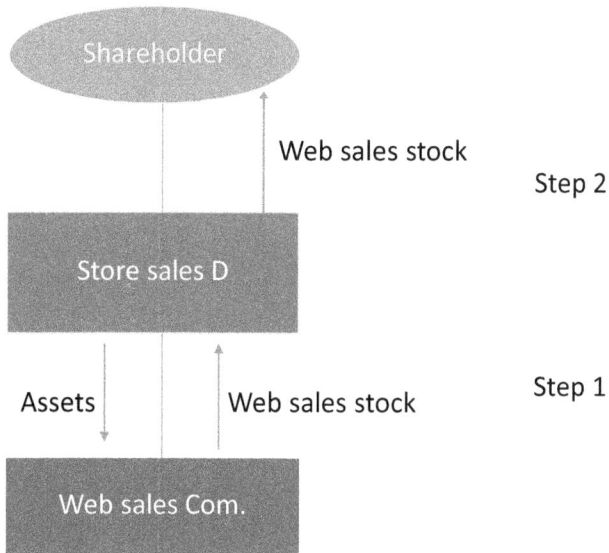

Figure 9.10 Expansion of an existing business

Expansion of an Existing Business

D Corporation was an automobile dealer for brand X who obtained a franchise to sell brand Y. D purchased the assets of an existing dealership selling brand Y and transferred the assets to Corporation C. Within 5 years of the acquisition, D Corporation distributed the C stock to its shareholders. The Service ruled that the acquisition of the Y dealer assets was an expansion of an existing trade or business and thus the 5 years of business history associated with the X dealership carried over to the Y dealership and, therefore, the active conduct of a trade or business for a section 355 distribution was satisfied. Therefore, the distribution of the C stock to the D shareholders could qualify as nontaxable under section 355. See Rev. Rul. 2003-18, 2003-7 I.R.B. 467 (Figure 9.11).

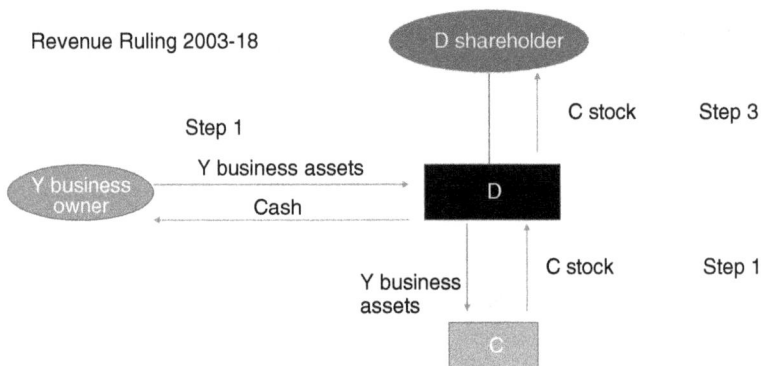

Figure 9.11 Expansion of an existing business

Predecessor and Successor

Shareholder X owns 100 percent of P Corporation, and shareholder Y owns 100 percent of D Corporation. P merges into D in an "A" reorganization. Less than 2 years after the merger, X and Y owned 10 percent and 90 percent, respectively, of the stock of D. D then contributed in a section 368(a)(1)(D) reorganization, one of the former P assets to C, P's wholly owned subsidiary, for additional C stock, and then distributes C to its shareholders pro rata (Figure 9.12).

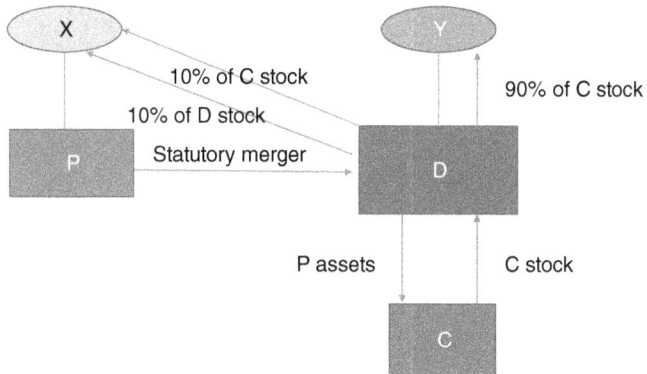

Figure 9.12 Predecessor and successor

P was the predecessor, and C was the successor. As a result of the transfers, P's shareholders went from 100 percent owners to a 10 percent owner of the P assets transferred to C. Therefore, if the merger and distribution are part of a plan, the distribution by D is a taxable under section 355(e) because, in effect, the P shareholders decreased their ownership interest in the P assets transferred from 100 percent to 10 percent.

Section 355(d)

Case 1

A has owned his 40 percent stock in D Corporation for at least 5 years, and D has owned 100 percent of the C stock for at least 5 years. B has owned his 60 percent of the D stock less than 5 years before he received 100 percent of the C stock in a split-off. The D stock B purchased within 5 years of the distribution is "disqualified stock." B owned 100 percent of the C stock after the distribution, and the C stock was received in respect of his disqualified stock in D Corporation. Therefore, under section 355(d), the distribution is taxable to D, but is not taxable to B. See House Report No.101-964, p. 1088 (Figure 9.13).

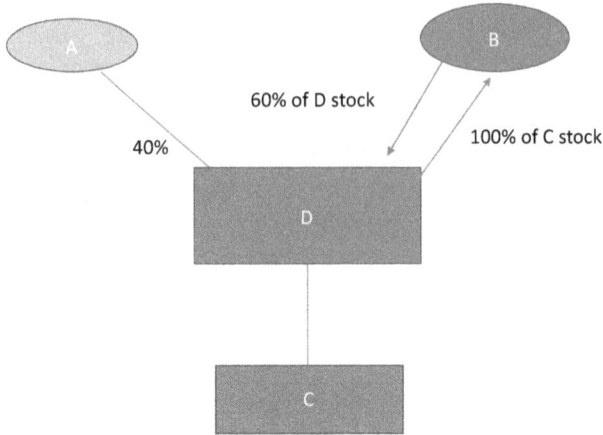

Figure 9.13 Section 355(d)

Case 2

Assume that B had owned his D stock for at least 5 years before the C stock was distributed to B, but A had purchased his D stock less than 5 years before the distribution to B. The redemption of B's stock caused A's interest in D to increase to 100 percent of the D stock. Because A owned his D stock less than 5 years and after the distribution he owns at least 50 percent of the D stock, the distributing corporation, he is a disqualified shareholder. Therefore, the distribution to A is taxable to D under section 355(d).

Section 355(b)(2)(D)

T Corporation had owned the S Corporation stock for at least 5 years when P Corporation purchased 100 percent of the T stock. Within 5 years of P's purchase of the T stock, T distributed the S stock to P and P distributed to its shareholders the S stock. The distribution of the S stock to the P shareholders is taxable under section 355(b)(2)(D) because P had received the S stock as a distribution within 5 years of the purchase of the T stock. This is a violation of a general section 355 requirement, and therefore, the general rules for corporate distributions apply. See Rev. Rul. 89-37, 1989-11 I.R.B. 4. The P shareholders have dividend income equal to the value of the S stock. (Figure 9.14).

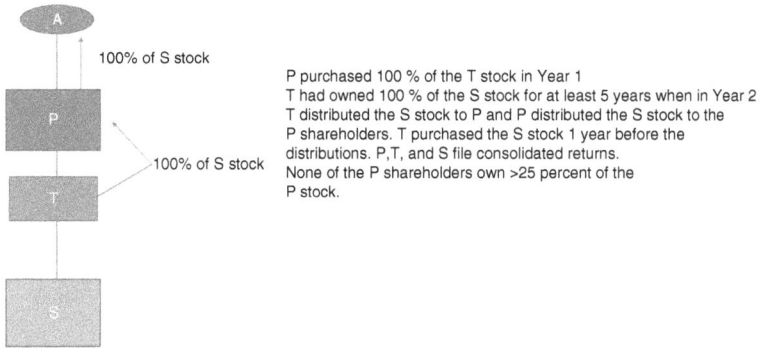

A

100% of S stock

P

100% of S stock

T

S

P purchased 100 % of the T stock in Year 1
T had owned 100 % of the S stock for at least 5 years when in Year 2
T distributed the S stock to P and P distributed the S stock to the
P shareholders. T purchased the S stock 1 year before the
distributions. P,T, and S file consolidated returns.
None of the P shareholders own >25 percent of the
P stock.

Figure 9.14 Sections 355(b)(2)(D) and 355(d)

The distribution of S to P also violates section 355(d) because control of S was distributed to a disqualified shareholder. However, section 355(d) is only relevant if the transactions otherwise satisfy section 355, which is not true if the section 355(b)(2)(D) conditions are not satisfied. In essence, section 355(b)(2)(D) overrides section 355(d).

Leveraged Spin-Off

G owned 100 percent of the H stock. G and H Corporations have actively conducted businesses for 5 years when H borrowed cash, which it transferred along with other assets to S for stock. H had remaining assets that were "unwanted" by G, but "wanted" by R. G made a section 355 distribution of the H stock to its shareholders within 2 years G's receipt of the S stock. The formation of S and the distribution by H of the S stock to G were all internal (within the control group of corporations) and not subject to section 355. Then G distributed the H stock to the G shareholders which was subject to the section 355 requirements. Assuming all of the general section 355 requirements were satisfied, the distribution of the H stock to the G shareholders would be nontaxable. However, the exchange by the G shareholders of the H stock for R stock would be subject to section 355(e). Unless the G shareholders owned at least 50 percent of the R stock after the H for R stock exchange, G is taxable on the distribution of the H stock. If the distribution is taxable under section 355(e), H can make a section 336(e) election to have H recognize its gain as though it sold its assets and write-up bases in its assets and the H shareholders will not be required to recognize gain (Figure 9.15).

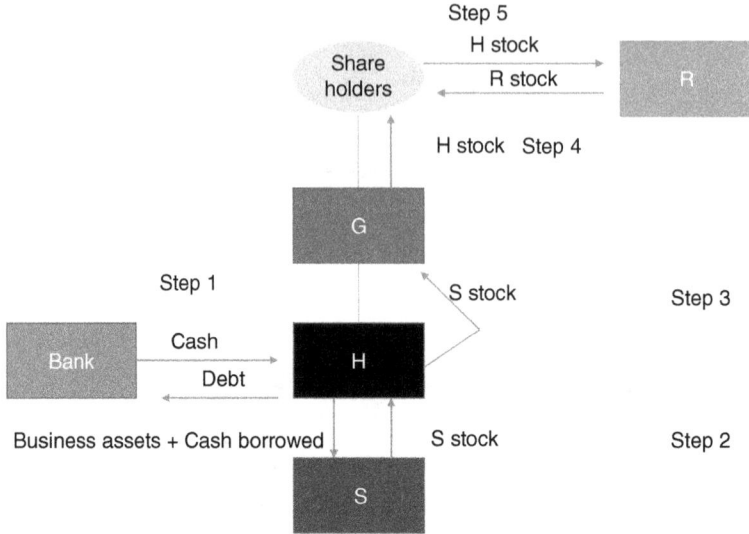

Figure 9.15 Leveraged spin-off

The leveraging aspect of the transactions is that S has retained the borrowed cash, and G has access to the borrowed cash because S is G's subsidiary, but H retained the obligation to pay the liability when it left the GHS group of corporations.

Carve-Out

For good business reasons, P will spin off S Corporation. P has owned S more than 5 years. Before P distributes the S stock, S declares a dividend payable to P in the form of a note payable. P and S file consolidated returns, and therefore, the dividend is not income but reduces P's basis in S. Also, before the distribution, S issued new stock to the general public, reducing P's interest in S to 80 percent. S used the cash to redeem the note payable to P, and P distributed its 80 percent of the S stock to the P shareholders. The distribution of S stock satisfies section 355 and, therefore, is nontaxable to P and its shareholders. The economic results are the same as if P sold 20 percent of S and did not recognize gain and then distributed the remaining 80 percent. (Figure 9.16).

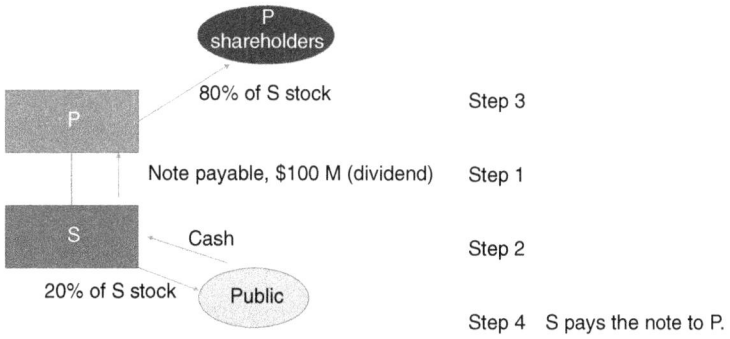

Figure 9.16 Carve-out

About the Author

W. Eugene Seago, Ph.D. J.D., is the Virginia Tech Curling Professor Emeritus of Accounting. He received his Ph.D. and J.D. degrees from the University of Georgia. He is a member of the Virginia Bar and the American Institute of Certified Public Accountants. He is the former editor of the Journal of Legal Tax Research and president of the American Taxation Association. In 2008 he was named the Outstanding Tax Educator by the EY Education Foundation.

He has authored or co-authored over 200 taxation articles, and is the author of *The Tax Aspects of Acquiring a Business* (Business Expert Press, 2018).

Index

OTHER TITLES IN OUR FINANCIAL ACCOUNTING, AUDITING, AND TAXATION COLLECTION

Mark Bettner, Bucknell University, Michael Coyne, Fairfield University, and Rob Sawyers, North Carolina State University (Taxation Topics), *Editors*

Concise and Applied Business Books

The Collection listed above is one of 30 business subject collections that Business Expert Press has grown to make BEP a premiere publisher of print and digital books. Our concise and applied books are for...

- Professionals and Practitioners
- Faculty who adopt our books for courses
- Librarians who know that BEP's Digital Libraries are a unique way to offer students ebooks to download, not restricted with any digital rights management
- Executive Training Course Leaders
- Business Seminar Organizers

Business Expert Press books are for anyone who needs to dig deeper on business ideas, goals, and solutions to everyday problems. Whether one print book, one ebook, or buying a digital library of 110 ebooks, we remain the affordable and smart way to be business smart. For more information, please visit **www.businessexpertpress.com**, or contact **sales@businessexpertpress.com**.